# THE ROLE OF BIOETHICS IN EMOTIONAL PROBLEMS

Following up from the previous book, *Human Emotions and the Origins of Bioethics*, this volume focuses on four psychological problems, anxiety, narcissism, restlessness, and emotional numbness, and explores how these problems influence bioethical issues and what bioethics can do to fix them.

*The Role of Bioethics in Emotional Problems* presents a phenomenological exploration of emotional intention and describes how one's choices can determine a better relationship to themselves and their community. Not only does this book provide the reader with an exhaustive account of the philosophical and psychological meaning of practical intentionality within Husserl's phenomenology, but it also applies Husserl's ethics to contemporary studies of human emotions and bioethical problems. Offering a non-reductionist model for an interdisciplinary inquiry into an emotional experience, it integrates clinical practice and articulates foundational knowledge of human emotional life at a professional level.

Aimed at students of philosophy, psychology, psychotherapy, and bioethics, this book is a unique phenomenological dialogue between these disciplines on emotional well-being.

**Susi Ferrarello** is assistant professor at California State University, East Bay and a philosophical counselor.

# THE ROLE OF BIOETHICS IN EMOTIONAL PROBLEMS

## A Phenomenological Analysis of Intentions

*Susi Ferrarello*

Routledge
Taylor & Francis Group

NEW YORK AND LONDON

First published 2021
by Routledge
605 Third Avenue, New York, NY 10158

and by Routledge
2 Park Square, Milton Park, Abingdon, Oxon, OX14 4RN

*Routledge is an imprint of the Taylor & Francis Group, an informa business*

*Library of Congress Cataloging-in-Publication Data*
A catalog record for this title has been requested

ISBN: 978-0-367-65420-7 (hbk)
ISBN: 978-0-367-67461-8 (pbk)
ISBN: 978-1-003-13138-0 (ebk)

Typeset in Bembo
by MPS Limited, Dehradun

Xavier Letizia, the brother I met at the right time in life

# CONTENTS

# INTRODUCTION

What are emotions? What is their role in individual and societal well-being? To what extent does bioethics take emotions into consideration when new policies or decisive choices need to be made?

The founder of bioethics, Rensselaer van Potter, considered the understanding of emotional problems and individual behaviors as an essential layer of bioethics whose goal was to guarantee the sustainable survival of our species and planet. Yet, as I explained more in depth in my previous book *Human Emotions and the Origins of Bioethics* (2021), emotions seem to have been dismissed early on in the bioethical discourse because of the stigma that had gathered around them. I believe that since emotions are what makes us human, a bioethics that does not seriously take into account emotions is a bioethics for nonhumans, a discipline that is useless to us.

As I showed in *Human Emotions and the Origins of Bioethics* (2021), the dismissive attitude we inherited against emotions finds its roots in ancient philosophy and expresses itself loud and clear in the inhuman way in which we have treated different areas of our lives—from the environment to mental health, education to food, technology to professions. In the ancient history of philosophy, emotions are considered to be what makes us similar to animals. It would appear that what we share with animals, and what led Pythagoras to suppose that they had a special kinship with us (Dicaearchus in Porphyry, 1965, *VP* 19), is not intellect, as some have supposed (Sorabji 1993, 78 and 208), but rather the ability to feel emotions such as pleasure and pain. Democritus' answer to Heraclitus—"it's difficult to fight against thumos (loosely translatable with spirit) but it is the job of the rational human being to conquer it" (DK, 68 B 236)—shows us how "fighting against" emotions seems to be seen as the right way to a healthy life. On the contrary, I believe that any form of emotional repression or dismissive attitude toward emotions generates problems that severely hinder our well-being.

Hence, in this book, which I consider as the natural continuation of *Human Emotions and the Origins of Bioethics* (2021), I will discuss some of the most common emotional problems we face in our daily lives. Since enough attention has been paid to severe psychiatric disorders, I decided to focus here on the small emotional problems that cloud our judgment in life. I wanted to show how simple daily emotional problems that affect large segments of the population to varying degrees—such as emotional numbness, loneliness, and restlessness—can influence our decisions, and negatively impact our individual and collective well-being. In each chapter, I will show how each of these emotional problems is often sustained by a problematic intentional structure and how bioethics can help us to repair these intentional problems and the structural conditions that sustain them.

Intentionality is one way, but not the only one, to access a description of the emotional problems I tackled in the present book. Since in this book I discuss some of the cases I have encountered during my philosophical practice, and since I often apply a phenomenological approach with my clients, intentionality appeared to me as the best way to access the description of these lived experiences.

In the first chapter, I discussed the problem of narcissism and its impact on the environment. The environment is, also, an important key to explaining the emotional problems involved in narcissistic patterns. In fact, the detachment from the environment generates a disengaged attitude toward those feelings, emotions, and sensations that connect the individual to a shared sense of reality. I explained why a bioethics that aims at communal survival should take into consideration the problems raised by a society in which narcissism is accepted and normalized. For this reason, I proposed an interpretation that compares narcissistic traits to a diffused health problem, like a flu. Similar to a flu, suffering often from narcissistic patterns can be draining for oneself and others as it increases the sense of loneliness and promotes carelessness toward loved ones, coworkers, and the general environment. To describe the common narcissistic patterns I used Greek and Roman mythology, specifically Ovid's interpretation of Narcissus' myth and the little known myth of Cassius and Mariam. Then, I considered the main treatments used to heal people suffering from "the narcissistic flu." This excursus served me to prepare the ground for the intentional approach I propose to use as a remedy against this flu. The most important finding emerging from the intentional approach is that real healing is possible when reconnection with the environment, the intimate one in the first place, occurs. A reconnection to the passive syntheses of their present and past life, including especially the painful memories that blocked the constitution of a safe reality, is particularly effective. This reconnection represents, in fact, the best way to reconstruct the foundation of their present life and assign real meanings and values to their lived experience. Reconnection with their present and past environment helps narcissists to fill the void left from the disruption of the intimate space caused by the lack of parental (or primary caregivers') care. Giving them the tools to look at that space and find valuable essences in there is the first step to readjust their intentional activity to a stronger ego. Finally, in the last part of the chapter, I analyzed the impact that narcissism has in politics, science, and the environment with the hope that more interdisciplinary studies on this problem will follow.

In the second chapter, I examined the emotional geography of anxiety in order to show the way in which the emotional blockage triggered by anxiety has the power to annihilate the environment and transform its reality into a black hole in which the individuals disappear. Through the analysis of a case study I have shown the steps that the individual can take to recover the interconnection between their body and the environment and overcome the anxious state. The steps involve an intentional reconnection of body and mind, as well as an unconditional acceptance from the individual of their psychophysical vulnerability. In the second part of the chapter, I examined the intersubjectivity of the physical and virtual environments. I have explained how schools, for example, can increase the quality of care toward their students by paying attention to their emotional view of the learning space. This approach revealed to be particularly helpful for disadvantaged students who were suffering from anxiety and anger issues. I examined how less tangible intersubjective environments such as the virtual space of a chat room or the virtual medical office of a doctor can be both beneficial and detrimental to our well-being. Hence, a bioethics meant to foster a good quality of life needs to take into consideration these emotional and environmental factors; any form of detachment from the environment increases the chances of a poor quality of life.

The third chapter focused on the paradox of exclusion which characterizes emotional numbness. Traumatic experiences might lead one to feel excluded. This primal exclusion reflects on a deeper form of exclusion according to which the same person who was once excluded excludes, then, themselves from their own intimate space and starts living a life according to an external social script. This chapter showed how this dynamic reflects not only on the level of personal life, creating emotional numbness and eventually depression, but also on a social and biological level: a water crisis or antisocial behaviors in the professional life are some of the examples presented in this chapter. Cases that range from personal life to medical dilemmas were used to show what kind of reality emotional numbness gives shape to and how that impacts the life we conduct in our environment. Breaking emotional numbness through reconnection with one's own intimate life could be conducive to recuperating one's vitality, both in their personal and social lives. The phenomenological use of reduction was proposed as a method to shed light on the complex time and space reality of the hurtful emotions that hide behind the primal exclusion.

In the fourth chapter, I discussed a positive and negative form of restlessness. Described in philosophy as a form of inner energy that encourages us to become who we are, restlessness can also be a destructive force. When we lose our sense of home, restlessness can lead us to do things of which we are not proud or we feel foreign from our real way of being. It happens in life that we feel disconnected from our center and miss the place in which we can recharge and feel in charge of our well-being. Missing that core, which can be the literal home in which we feel safe or that inner space that we can trust as the ultimate resource to be who we really are, decenters ourselves from our own system and from the system of life in which we live. Losing that center means losing our ability to be subject of and to our acts and to respond for what we do in front of others that summon us to action. Recovering this center becomes even harder when we lose control over our well-being as we get trapped in the particularism of different health systems that tell us what is good for us without us being able to have a say in what feels congruent to our concrete being. For this reason, in the second part of the chapter I discussed the case of Eka, a Molucca woman, who was living through a moment of intense distress and was cured with medications that intensified her problem. This case of Ulysses Syndrome shows how the loss of her home generated a series of problems in the intentional acts with which this woman expressed herself and her belongingness to the hosting culture. Here collective intentions were often incongruent with the concrete fulfillment she expected and needed to constitute meaning and value of her own. Yet, since she was a newcomer, her system of thinking, as usual, was completely decentered from her core and she had to employ twice the energy to reconstruct it. She had literally no energy left to recalibrate the congruence between her own intentions and her responses in relation to the collective ones. To cure this negative restlessness which generated the chronic problems we labeled under the Ulysses Syndrome, it was necessary to bring congruence in her life so that she could find a home where to feel safe. At the beginning of a migratory journey, it felt safer for her to blend in the collectivity and trust that this collective compound will be able to produce the meanings she needed to survive. I believe this is part of the adaptive process and the desire to fit. Yet, this emergency behavior needs to be shifted toward a subjective responsibility of one's own acts, meanings, and values, in order to bring that congruence from which life can make sense. Fortunately, in the case of Eva, her home system understood the roots of her distress before her doctors could and did all that was possible to recenter her in her new system creating a bridge between her old and new system which brought the congruence that was needed for her to feel at home, again.

# 1

# NARCISSISTS MISSING THEIR ENVIRONMENT

## Introduction

This chapter and the two that will follow will discuss the psychophysical consequences of disconnection of individuals from each other and their environment as a result of a worldview informed by substance dualism, scientism, and reductionism.[1] In these four chapters I will use my experience as a philosophical counselor and as a scholar in phenomenology to describe four common psychophysical phenomena—such as loneliness, anxiety, emotional numbness, and restlessness—that strongly impact the well-being of the individuals and their environment. Even though these phenomena are not considered among the most disruptive emotional disorders, they are very common and plague daily the life of a large number of people. As Potter showed (more on this in my *Human Emotions and the Origins of Bioethics,* chapter 1), it is very important for bioethics to address these problems since bioethics is the discipline that aims at preserving the well-being of our species in our ecosystem and our inner balance is essential to make the right choices in the right direction.

In this chapter I will examine how emotional intentionality operates in the intimate life of narcissists and generates a primal sense of loneliness. Focusing on the notion of volitional body (Husserl, 2002) and interaffectivity (Fuchs & De Jaegher, 2009), I will investigate the intentional structure of the major emotional choices that shape narcissist's emotional intimate lives. Henceforth, the chapter will be organized in the following manner. First, it will briefly discuss narcissism through Greek and Latin myths. Second, it will consider what are the best ways to treat narcissistic problematic patterns in individuals and their impact on the environment; in particular, I will use the notion of intentionality and intimacy to look through the problem. Finally, I will move to the description of the narcissistic wound as it expresses itself through intentional and interaffective dynamics in the personal life, politics, science, and the natural environment. The goal is to understand what bioethics can do to prevent people heavily affected by narcissistic traits from harming themselves and the society in which we all live.

I believe that such clarification of the interaffective intentionality would increase narcissists' chances to be rehabilitated to a healthier life. Removing the "intentional blockage" that prevents them from exploring the content of their lived-experience would restore an interaffective space conducive to a more flourishing intimate life with their loved ones.

## 1.1 The Narcissistic Flu

"It's all about them," "Run, as fast as you can!," "How to know that you're dating a narcissist"—these are just a few of the mediatic "witch-hunting" titles that reference narcissism and can currently be found all over the internet.[2] Although narcissistic behavior can be highly intoxicating, I believe it is important to maintain a position of compassionate understanding so as to be able to look at the reasons behind its development and to be able to recognize the narcissistic traits that hide in ourselves.

In my work as a philosophical counselor I came to the idea that getting stuck in narcissistic patterns is a sort of emotional flu that can affect each one of us to different degrees. This flu, like any flu, is caused by a variety of environmental factors that impact us throughout our daily lives and the way in which we respond to them. While stricken with a normal flu our head would feel congested and our nose would be running preventing us from breathing well. Similarly to this, while stricken with a narcissistic emotional flu the lack of access to our intimacy would congest our emotional breathing. This access, in fact, gets clogged and leaves us with a strong sense of loneliness and powerless rage that reduces our vital breath. It might happen, in fact, that external factors impact important areas of life with which we identify and through which we gain the ability to connect with an intimate sense of self.

For the sake of clarity, let us use a practical case. A couple undergoes a devastating loss; the father of the husband unexpectedly dies. The wife is supportive and understanding during the first year after the loss. Then, something changes. She laments that the husband is becoming more and more detached and distant. The safe space of their love feels threatened to her. An important area from which she used to get validation and intimate connection is shaken maybe in a way that resonates with previous traumas. Without considering that her husband's mourning is still occurring, her instinctive reaction to this threat is to disconnect even more from her husband (for the fear of being abandoned first) and oneself (for the fear of questioning herself and proving herself wrong). Hence, she finds refuge in an empty and very fragile space of herself from which she demands love and attention without having the energy to calmly find a way in which they can both meet these demands.

The feeling that accompanies this demand is, generally, a very scary one—there is the anxiety of disappearing if the demands are not met (which is quite likely when one reaches this space of loneliness), as if the whole sense of self would be shattered and scattered everywhere. The anxiety behind this reaction is the fear of disappearing. So, the responsibility of coming to existence as a person connected to others is all put on the shoulders of the husband in this case. Specifically, the wife demands from him to show her his love in this and that way—although these are rarely the ways in which the spell can be broken since this emotional flu can only be cured through real connection and warmth. She accuses the husband of being distant, cold, and detached without truly trying to be empathetic and compassionate toward him or herself. Both are stuck because they are in a place that is not real, it is a place of fearful anticipations and constant anxieties and, consequently, none of their efforts can be fully appreciated because it will be taunted by fear. In a place like this, she cannot find a way to take care of herself because her sense of self feels under attack and there are no ways to truly nurture it. She is experiencing a sort of emotional flu. She feels extremely lonely, incapable of being happy with what she has, and unable to connect with other people because she is too miserable. The sense of loneliness makes her feel even more abandoned and unsafe.

This sense of rageful loneliness, this feeling that the world owes her something because up to that point it has been unfair to her, is a red flag for the emotional flu. These feelings should be taken as if our nose is running or our head feels congested. I think that some narcissistic traits can be read as a sort of a flu that appears when the roads to our intimate life get clogged by the struggles of life. If the wife happens to be without a job, or sick, or in a foreign country it is possible that the momentary carelessness of the husband will be felt as more threatening because all the other accesses she had to herself are blocked and her only way to be is through his warmth and affection. I think that this form of self-righteous, frustrating loneliness can be used as a thermometer for this kind of fever and the cure is to reopen the access to intimacy by reconnecting life to the environment. The pill to take is finding the road to our intimate well-being and it can start by taking care of others: walking our dog, volunteering for a cause we like, calling a friend in need.

If we cannot be alone with ourselves without feeling excruciatingly lonely or unlucky, as if the world owes us something, then maybe the narcissism virus is circulating inside of us and clogging the access to our intimacy. In what follows I will write more about how to recover from this flu and how to access the road of intimacy by describing first the myth of Narcissus and then, the way in which a narcissist can gain back their access to a balanced intimate life.[3]

## 1.1.1 Narcissus and other Stories

*Am I the lover or beloved? Then why make love? Since I am what I long for, then my riches are so great they make me poor.*

(Ovid Metamorphoses, 3, 464)

The myth of Narcissus is by itself illustrative of the intentional problem lying at the basis of narcissistic traits. Narcissus was believed to be the son of the river god Cephissus and the nymph Lirope. As a river, his father's nature was elusive and distant; as a nymph, his mother Lirope was emotionally distant and carefree. Emotional detachment of the primary caregivers in early childhood is often indicated as one of the main reasons for the development of narcissistic traits (Kohut, 1971, 1977; Horton, 2011). The inability to establish meaningful emotional bonds at early stages of emotional development generates a void in which the child and, later on, the adult cultivates low self-esteem and a sense of restlessness that finds momentary peace only in validations of self-worth from external sources (Donaldson-Pressman and Pressman, 1994). The lack of attention from primary caregivers leads to a vicious circle in which the child mirrors the behavior of the caregivers. In fact, as they do not show curiosity about the child's life, similarly the child does not devote time or develop tools to explore its own qualities and talents. These are the ingredients for a miserable life whose healing can come only through metamorphosis.

Ovid's phantasy, for example, sees Narcissus transforming himself into a graceful flower; his metamorphosis is healing because it allows him to break with his old patterns and ground solid roots into a nurturing soil. Parthenios of Nicaea and Conon see him ending his life with suicide and, maybe less plausibly, Pausanias imagines Narcissus falling in love with his twin sister and starting a new life. Despite the differences, one common theme among these later interpretations of the myth is the disintegration of the image that Narcissus has of himself. Although Ovid's phantasy is more merciful than others' and leaves space for a healing metamorphosis after painful realization, for all these authors the way for Narcissus to recover is by breaking the parental patterns and healing through a metaphorical death.

In the myth, the fortune teller Thiresia foresaw Narcissus' problems and told his mother that Narcissus would have had an easier life if no realization about his own image had occurred. Outside the myth, studies have noticed how the percentage of narcissists seeking professional help is extremely low since they prefer to not know about their problem. Narcissists experience high anxiety in challenging their structure because their image is a depositary of a whole life-system that they do not want to challenge (Muslin et al., 1985) even if they feel "the deepest anxiety a person can experience" (Kohut, 1987, 9).

In fact, as the myth continues, revengeful goddesses punish Narcissus' vanity by obliging him to this realization. Having refused the love of several nymphs, Aphrodite and Nemesis, goddesses of lust and revenge, trick him into seeing his own appearance in the reflection of a lake. Echo, one of the nymphs whom he had refused was still hiding in the forest after his rejection. Her body became a fading voice that could only repeat the last words of what others uttered aloud. Initially, Narcissus was pleased to hear her echoing his own words but with time he lost interest in her as he felt lonely with her. In the end, Narcissus got lost in himself, and Echo evanesced in him.

This tragic node of the myth mirrors, once again, the reality of dating a narcissist. The great enthusiasm and excitement that the narcissist experiences for the new partner are often followed by a sense of boredom and discontent. Having a relationship with a narcissist can be extremely draining for the partner because, like Echo, a partner's life can factually fade away in the narcissists' ongoing demands. The integrity of the partner's personality is so challenged by the blindness of the narcissistic partner that it tends to vanish into an ethereal invisible space (Campbell et al., 2002).

For this reason, as the story recounts, the two goddesses wanted to avenge the nymph and the other lovers to whom he caused pain. Aphrodite cast a spell on him: he would reflect on himself and fall in love with his own image. At this point of the story we find Narcissus, intent on looking at his own reflection in the water. This point is quite problematic, Ovid does not tell us if Narcissus is attracted to his own image or if the horror of what he sees freezes him; in both cases the result is that he cannot go anywhere else and interact with anyone other than himself. He is a slave to a mutable external reflection of himself that leaves him alone every time he moves. Narcissus is condemned to be lonely because of his desire to be loved. The only love of which he is capable is superficial as it is bound to a fictional mimicry of him; this makes him crave real love even more. As he tries to love he experiences more vulnerability and loneliness because he cannot reach anything substantial in himself. The image that he cherishes disappears every time he moves or tries to touch it without ever offering him that intimate connection he is desperately looking for. There is just him and nothing new is projected around him. Narcissus' wound cannot be healed and Aphrodite's punishment is fully accomplished. Reflection is a transformational lethal process for him. At the end of the myth, Narcissus dies or, according to Ovid's version, transforms itself into a beautiful flower.

In real life, people with narcissistic traits and personality disorder lack the emotional tools that would allow them to achieve a healthy reconnection with their feelings. It is difficult for them to truly reflect on themselves because they lack the empathetic drive to feel compassion for themselves. So, reflection can touch only the surface of their being. Their sense of self is built on a fleeting image reflected in how others see them or reified into material objects. Hence, they are extremely vulnerable to criticisms from others although at the same time they pretend to be better than those same people (e.g., Campbell et al., 2002; Gabriel et al., 1994) and unique in comparison (Emmons, 1987), which might be associated with a high degree of psychological entitlement (Campbell et al., 2004). Any personal negative remark would be felt as a personal attack to their whole being, as if the other would want to make them disappear. They feel extremely empty because they cannot establish any contact with their emotions, so they try to counterbalance this emptiness with grandiose fantasies and a cult of the ego. This appears to them as the best strategy to restate their existence.[4] If they manage to reflect fully on themselves and to reach the deepest part of who they are then their sense of self will dissolve and a healing metamorphosis will occur, as in Ovid's interpretation of the myth.

### 1.1.2 The Myth of Cassius and Mariam

Similarly, a lesser known myth recounts the story of another "Narcissus" named Cassius, a young handsome man spoiled by a nymph who is desperately in love with him. Like Narcissus and Echo, these two do not make a good pair together. She provides him with any goods he might desire. Any whim or wish of his is satisfied by her but nothing for him is ever enough. A day arrives when he is demanding something that she cannot give him. He feels very lonely. His nymph is not enough for him, so he starts wandering around the forest in search of some company. There he sees her, Mariam, a young woman who is crossing the lake in her small boat. He greets her and she greets him back from afar. She was going back to her garden, she tells him when he interrogates her. "I want to come with you" he says "But you don't know me" she replies. "We will get to know each other. For now, please, take me with you." he begs. She accepts but with one condition: "It took me a long time to take care of my garden, growing my food, and creating a comfortable place for me and my people. I will take you with me if you respect my garden and give me a baby." "I will give you a baby," he says without blinking. "This means that you will take care of everything when I'm with the baby and you will work to provide for us; you will play music to comfort me and the baby when we are in pain." "Yes, I will do all this", he says again without thinking twice. "Ok, then. Be aware that once this boat sails, you will not be able to come back to your life as it was. You will start your new life with me and the life as you lived it before will cease."

This last condition is terrifying for Cassius. Feeling his hesitation, the nymph, still in love with him, takes her chances and starts offering him even more gifts. She materializes in front of him in the shape of a beautiful woman, Miriam, looking so similar to Mariam that he forgets about Mariam. They spend one year together enjoying every kind of lust. One day, though, the memory of what he has missed comes back to haunt him. He wants to find Mariam and accept her offer. Yet, he is now too late. When the two meet she tells him that she has found a man and they have a baby together. Cassius, desperate for this loss and the sense of loneliness, gives up on his life and died by suicide.

This story, similar to the previous one, portrays a perfectly looking young man who is missing something important in his life—the connection with himself. We do not know much about his childhood, but we know that his world, similarly to Narcissus', is populated only by two-dimensional persons who exist only to serve his needs and whose lives are almost completely invisible to him. They are there only to mirror him in the way he prefers the most. Although this is momentarily pleasing, it leaves him with a growing sense of desperation and emptiness that pushes him to try to take part in the real world. Yet, he does not have the tools to endure in this world because he cannot give up on the image he has of himself; the image is all he has and giving that up would mean to die. Mariam's condition to leave his old self behind is dreadful. Exploring a new real life would be a lethal threat to his very existence. Although dissolving the old patterns and enduring the transformation seems to be the only way to heal, taking that chance would mean to kill the image behind which his fragile ego hides and shields itself. According to Greek and Latin mythology, it seems that there is no escape from this existential situation. Narcissists are doomed to an excruciating loneliness unless they are willing to kill themselves, that is, to transform completely themselves and their lives.

Plato's *Symposium* finds a more optimistic solution to the problem. According to Sygminton (1993), Aristophanes' speech on the androgens is a way to figure out the narcissistic problem. The split that takes place at the very origin of their creation is a metaphor for the traumatized event that splits the young life of these individuals because of the absence of their parents. In the myth the androgens were split into males and females because Zeus was jealous of their completeness. Similarly, adults presenting narcissistic traits feel incomplete and empty.

To heal this sense of incompleteness, the solution presented by Aristophanes is love. Finding your own half can help incomplete persons to feel whole. Often, the problem is that narcissists have great difficulties in experiencing real intimacy and love for others (for a recent review, see Morf & Rhodewalt, 2001). For this reason, I propose a method that aims at developing intimacy through intentional reconnection and compassionate acceptance of their own limits.

## 1.2 Treatments

At the moment, it seems very difficult to find a specific approach to treat pathological narcissism, which is no longer considered a personality disorder according to the fifth edition of the DSM, V, 2020. In the mid-1980s, Dr. Young developed a schema therapy to help narcissists to become aware of the behavioral pattern that underlies their mental condition. On this line, Johnson (1994), as well, thought that successful treatments should have required for narcissists to accept their own vulnerability and mature awareness toward their own behaviors. These approaches are still in use today.

The acceptance implied by these two procedures might lead at first to a strong sense of depression and sadness due to the newly gained sense of responsibility toward their own actions, but then a sense of completeness follows because the scattered parts of their personality are fully integrated. According to this approach, if integration occurs, maybe by creating a trustworthy relationship with the therapist, then actual healing could be possible. In the new relationship, in fact, the client can allow herself to feel her own feelings without the fear of parental judgment. Murray-Jobsis (1990a, 1990b, 1990c) showed how the new relationship might uncover a new sense for the boundaries between internal and external bodies (more on this in my *Human Emotions and the Origins of Bioethics,* chapter 5 and in the next section) that involves a different acceptance of an imperfect world and its surprises. To this purpose, Baker (1981) has also developed hypnotic techniques and self psychology based on the work of Mahler (1968). He invented exercises that allow the client to come back to a preverbal framework and recreate, there, new corrective experiences for the present. In particular, his fifth, sixth, and seventh exercises have the goal of reinforcing the presence of the therapist as a "good object"; the object constancy that the client lacked during their upbringing is replaced by the therapist who gives them the key to take part in an imperfect but surprising world. The seventh exercise addresses integrating positive and negative experiences while the therapist helps the client to get rid of the bad objects. In that sense, fantasy and imagination, more than meditation, can help the narcissistic client to reinforce constancy. Baker also emphasized the importance of empathy as a way for the therapist to help the patient to build an observing ego. The use of hypnotic techniques such as the affect bridge (Watkins, 1971), future projections (Phillips & Frederick, 1992), an assortment of other ego-strengthening techniques (Frederick & McNeal, 1999), and Ego State Therapy (Watkins & Watkins, 1987) might reduce the course of treatment from the usual two to three years to a little over one year.

Yet, I believe that whenever life events threaten one of the bridges to our intimacy and our sense of self (or at least the image with which we identify ourselves) the narcissistic wound that is in all of us becomes the potential focus of infection for the narcissistic flu to develop. In what follows I propose to combine the positive aspects of the abovementioned treatments into an intentionality oriented approach in order to create a maintenance treatment against this flu throughout life. Self-acceptance, ego-strengthening, and unfolding the feelings around the traumatic experience are possible by reconnecting with the intentionality of one's own actions. Grounding the narcissists to their own body as a part of a larger system is a fruitful way to overcome painful blockages and recover intimacy. From a bioethical point of view, helping society to reduce narcissism would direct us for a wiser use of the common resources and a growth of solidarity.

### 1.2.1 The Intentional Connection to the Environment

As shown in my *Human Emotions and the Origins of Bioethics,* chapter 3, passive intentionality represents the very first form of affective interconnection between an individual and the environment. The primordial way with which we exist is through affections. In my *Human Emotions and the Origins of Bioethics,* chapters 2 and 3, we described how the undifferentiated matter of nature organizes itself through two orders of passive syntheses, one spontaneous and the other non-spontaneous. In the spontaneous one,[5] the pairing process synthesizes data according to a principle of homogeneity that brings together matter of similar nature (Hua-Mat IV, Hua XVI) which speaks to us through affections (Hua XI). For example, my body is affected by a lack of food and feels hungry. Lower feelings will alert me (my volitional body) that there is a lack of energy in my body and if my volitional body does not make a timely decision about what needs to be done a higher feeling might take up that same alert in the form of tiredness, anger, or sadness. In that case a non-spontaneous synthesis takes place in which the affection of my hunger wakes my subjectivity through the volitional body and stirs the emotions that force me to feel my body. Then, it is up to my subjectivity (that is, the position that my ego has taken in relation to that matter, *Stellungnahme*) to make sense of what the body is experiencing. The very basic affection that connects my body to the undifferentiated matter of the environment speaks to my volitional body and incites it to make meanings, decisions, or even constitute values around the given interaffective experience. One's life is constituted on the basis of these interaffective syntheses that connect our bodies to the undifferentiated biological matter that shapes us into who we are.

As Lewin (1935) noticed, the tired body is more susceptible to affections and lower feelings than the awakened body, the drunk body more susceptible than the sober body, etc. The sympathetic nervous system that regulates the basic functions of my body is more receptive to the information provided by lower feelings, while the parasympathetic, which is in command of flight-fight signals, prompts the volitional body to immediate decisions by the elaboration of higher feelings such as fear or rage. Lower feelings have the task to communicate to us how the matter of our body is being affected and emotions are the way in which our whole being is moved to a specific direction (decision) according to the communication we sensed (sensations) in the feeling (more on this point in my *Human Emotions and the Origins of Bioethics,* chapters 2 and 3). As Ekman et al. (1972) remarked, feeling one's heart pound in fear raises one's anxiety, feeling one's cheeks burn with shame increases the painful experience of exposure and humiliation, and so on. Lower and higher feelings (pain/anxiety, hunger/rage) are the medium of the passive intentionality that operates on the basic level of affections. Ignoring affections, feelings, sensations, and emotions is the cause of severe psychological and physical problems because it cuts a person off from their own life and vitality. Being in contact with one's own fear, for instance, would not be possible if one is disconnected from the feelings of bodily tension or trembling, a beating of the heart, a shortness of breath, or a tendency to withdraw. The sensations generated by affections and communicated to us through feelings and emotions are a key to maintaining contact with who we really are and truly care for ourselves. The answer (more on this in the next section) that our volitional body gives to these affections is motivated by the social and familiar environment in which the person lives. Detached parents teach their children to ignore their own emotions; this teaching leads to establishing a shallow connection with themselves and their environment.

As Lowen wrote "narcissism describes both a psychological and cultural condition" (1983, 5). The value and meaning invested on one's image are "understandable" within "a society that sacrifices the natural environment for profit and power betrays its insensitivity to human needs" (1983, 5). Detachment from the environment causes detachment from one's own reality and the truthfulness of one's own body. Our parents are not the only caregivers we have in our life; society as a whole is the way in which we are introduced to life and we learn to take care of ourselves and each other. As Lowen rightly wrote: "The narcissism of the individual parallels that of the culture. We shape our culture according to our image and in turn we are shaped by that culture (...) And there is something crazy about a culture that pollutes the air, the waters, and the earth in the name of a higher standard of living" (1983, 5–6). Narcissism is a bioethical problem because it causes a progressive impoverishment of common resources out of greediness and a lower quality of interpersonal care through self-isolation. If bioethics is about the survival of Earth and the promotion of the quality of life, then it should work on this problem and its consequences on a societal level. A society that does not care for the natural environment would hardly care for its citizens because the most prioritized value would always be profit. Hence, this kind of society would be doomed to produce more narcissists because it will not provide families with the sufficient support to raise their children in a healthy environment (space to play, green areas, good food, psychological stability); parental leave would be discarded in favor of exploitation of the resources and more. This is all fertile soil for narcissism.

### 1.2.2 The Intentional Answer

The first consistent step that leads to the constitution of narcissistic traits at a very young age is characterized by a disconnection from one's own feelings and the environment that elicits them. (Lowen, 1983). Feelings, emotions, sensations are the *via regia* to understanding our interaction with reality; shutting them out means living in an alternative uprooted reality. Since this alternative reality ultimately becomes the main persistent cause of loneliness, as it mirrors the painful disruption of the familiar intimate space, the strategy of recreating a safe intimate space is essential to a successful recovery. From the start, the child does not choose to be detached from her parents but is passively obliged to accept that distance which can manifest in abuse, aloofness, and carelessness. The passive intentionality of the child has difficulty in generating an interconnection with her social and physical environment. It is as if the space around her is left empty and the child has been dropped in the middle of that emptiness. For this reason, as it is possible to prove in successful cases, as in McNeal (2003)[6] or McLean (2007),[7] helping the client to reinterpret and reintegrate the environment as a part of their own life and not as a hostile empty place is important for establishing a first, meaningful, constant connection with themselves.

As we saw in the previous section, passive intentionality is what defines us as a part of a social and biological system and it does not require an ego intervention in order to function—in fact, the subjectivity of the ego comes only at a very late stage of the process. Hence, to use a metaphor, if this biological and social system is missing, the passive intention runs low on oil and the engine risks burning.

We need to be part of a social, geographical, emotional, physical, imaginative environment in order to be and to become something. The more qualities this environment shows to us the richer would be our passive intentional life. Meditative or cognitive exercises that foster the client's ability to appreciate her environment can be useful to this purpose. As the case studies of McLean (2007) and McNeal (2003) show, one of the common traits that signify a healing process is taking place, in fact, is the client's recovered ability to finally appreciate nature and discover the beauty of a clear sky or a blossoming flower.

Yet, the reconnection to the passive intentionality is not enough to recover intimacy. Similar to people who suffered from traumatic experiences, narcissists have closed the access to their passive intentions because the emptiness of that space is too painful for them to accept and inhabit. As passive intentions delimit the space of our communal life, they represent the collective ground from which one's domestic, professional, and social life stem. In the case of narcissistic patterns, the people characterized by these traits find this space empty because the inadequate parental care has clogged the access to this area with fake tokens such as expensive objects, external interpersonal gratifications, fame, etc. For this reason, the role of the therapist is to help the client to reconnect with their own passive intentionality in order to heal the sense of primal exclusion from which the client is still suffering. The new relationship with the therapist and exercises directed at making the client feel like a part of her social, geographical, emotional, physical, imaginative environment, are useful to this goal.

The overall goal is to readjust the blocked interconnection of passive syntheses, practical intentionality, and active intentionality. Narcissists are not able to access the organic presence of their bodies. They have great difficulties in accepting their bodily flaws or even their own age. What these bodies are for them and what they do in their primal functioning (passive syntheses) feels almost shameful. This results in an inability to accept their own bodily functioning (practical intention) and assign them a meaning (active intention) that is commensurate to their possibility. Hence, the sense of grandiosity, the fixation on their image, and the sense of disconnection from others' bodies. For this reason, the awakening, represented by practical intention, has to be stimulated by exercises until it reaches the real ground of the passive syntheses and not the empty one created from the traumatic experience. At that point, when that reconnection occurs, it is possible to revisit the old places where the traumatic experiences took place. Through hypnotic, acceptance-based, mindful approaches, the intentional reconnection has the goal of recuperating the lower feelings and sensations that are still floating in the figurative rooms of the trauma and give them space to become emotions. Parenthetically, it is always important to remember that emotions, different from other forms of acts, live on a "timeless" level of time, they are not observable according to the linear sense of time of befores and afters. If particularly difficult emotions arise and are not faced, they do not disappear in the linearity of time, but they persist in a timeless now. They have to be lived in order to make space for new emotions to arise and fitting meanings to come. Narcissists feel emotional blockages and are often incapable of feeling pure joy or happiness because there is a long line of emotions waiting to be lived.

Hence, grounding the meanings (active intention) of their lives and their self-esteem on something unreal and untrustworthy (empty passive intentions) prevents any healing; only dealing with the still persistent and painful emotions would help an actual recovery. It is in the recovery from that sadness and sense of grief that a first entrance into real life can be discovered. A way to help narcissists' recovery is by mechanically adjusting the primary connection between passive syntheses and practical intentionality which involves taking responsibility for and accepting the organic nature of what they are and the grief that they have suffered. This acceptance is located in the specific space and environment of their primal life. In this step, the epoché should be used by the therapist and client to suspend any temptation to make ethical judgments or assign quick meanings to the complexity of passive syntheses.

What often happens at this stage is that ethical judgment gets in the way of true healing. In fact, it becomes easy to blame oneself and others for their own misery thus concealing the access to the constitution of any new meaning in life. Potentially neutral adjectives are transformed into ethically charged ones and create a blockage to the constitution of new meaning: weak instead of sad, selfish instead of alone, failing instead of trying. Covering up real sensations with ethical judgments is another way to block the interconnection between practical, passive, and active intentions. The counselor's goal is to create an ethically neutral space of acceptance around the arousal of each sensation so that lower feelings and sensations can arise freely and guide the therapist–client relationship toward a transformative healing process of sensations into emotions and then meaning and values.

Once this acceptance is completed and habitualized, then the client can proceed to the next step which consists of the actual constitution of meanings based on their affective experiences. At that point, meanings would be based on rounded, trustworthy, and solidly based experienced reality as opposed to the grandiose empty reality fancied as a shield to the traumatized ego. From there the client can start rebuilding a personal value system that will be at the basis of their new ethics and the way in which they want to embody their life in the real world. At that point, life will cease to be pointless, lonely, empty, or without surprises.

Of course, this process is extremely difficult and painful because it implies an actual dissolution of old structures on multiple levels. Yet, if it occurs, the renewal will be complete. The narcissist can transform herself into a more graceful and down-to-earth creature whose roots are safely protected by the "dirt" of the world, as the flower in Ovid's myth. The temptation to fall back into old habits would be continuously there as it is for any seasonal flu, but a way to recover from that sense of loneliness and desperation is possible.

## 1.3 Cases

In this second part of the chapter, I will present cases that show the large impact that narcissism has on our personal life, the sciences, politics, the environment, and common resources. This is the reason why I believe that emotional disorders have the same weight in bioethics as biotechnological dilemmas or difficult medical decisions.

### 1.3.1 Michael

When I was working as a philosophical counselor in Switzerland, I received an email request from a client. He asked me if we could use a free consultation appointment which I generally provide as a first appointment for people in financial need. That first email was followed by three more in which the client wanted to share with me, through links, his work. We scheduled a meeting first in person then online because the day before our meeting he warned me that he could not come. The meeting became a phone call. Since I could not see my client, the consultation was more difficult, and I knew that I had to be more careful in expressing my opinions in relation to what he was telling me. After five minutes of conversation Michael asked me, in apprehension, if I thought he was affected by a personality disorder—a question that I certainly cannot answer given my professional expertise and the very short time of our meeting. Michael is a foreigner in Switzerland, he is in his mid-thirties and has been living with a woman for five years. She was a year younger than him and they had been colleagues before becoming partners. Jasmine, his partner, met Michael when she was engaged to another man. After the two married, Michael realized he had feelings for her. For this reason, he resolved to talk to her and tell her that he could not see her again. She could not accept that and decided to break up with her newly married husband and start a new relationship with Michael. The two had lived together ever since. Michael contacted me because he was surprised about his bouts of rage and his grumpiness toward life. For example, Michael was passionate about cooking but found himself becoming furious when simple, cheap recipes did not meet his expectations. Since he got stuck in this narrative and did not know how to move forward I decided to ask him about his day. He told me that he was unemployed. He usually does not go out because he finds people stupid and he does not have anything in common with them. He said that he was quite well-read in psychology and recognized that, as a discipline, it studies outside body experiences, mysteries, and so on. His girlfriend and other people are incapable of meeting his educational and conversational standards, especially when it comes to entertaining an exchange on psychological topics. He told me about his romantic life. Before this partner, Jasmine, he said that he was not so nice toward girls. He had long stories but was never loyal to them. It was their fault if, in the end, he had to break up with each one of them. One for example was "behaving like a teenager" or another one had "a very annoying mother." In his relationship with Jasmine, he said, he had finally learnt what it meant to be with someone. Jasmine was very strong and caring. He did not say it openly but it was clear that she provided for him financially while he continued his studies. Although she never paid him compliments, which he found very disruptive for the couple, she was quite remarkable. Michael found it quite problematic that she would come home and not compliment his looks, making him feel unimportant and unattractive, did not want to engage in the intelligent conversations he wanted to have, and would not have satisfying sex with him. "She does not make me feel like I am desirable. Soon I have to look for someone else to feel like that again." When I asked him how intimacy is between the two of them, he told me that it was awful. She is always tired and stressed. "I told her to do sports but she does it for a couple of weeks and then she drops." When I asked him if he felt intimate with himself he said that he was very intimate. I think in the conversation the word intimate was meant by him as a polite replacement for sex. To give me the sense of how good the intimacy with himself was, he added, "I had to tell her that now to get aroused I think only about myself and keep her out of the picture. I make my own movie and she is not even in there." When I tried to propose to him ways for regaining intimacy with her, he turned down my suggestions, instead emphasizing his misery and the injustice in which he was living because his partner was too apathetic. No feelings or emotions of his were ever mentioned in the conversation. He objectified both his and his partner's bodies. He was surprised that his girlfriend did not react in an engaging way whenever he told her that "she had a great ass!" This first free consultation did not have, to date, any follow-up. When thinking back on the support I could have provided him, both to escape his loneliness and to gather new energy in his draining relationship, I am left with a strong sense of inadequacy.

At the end of our conversation, I showed him the connection between his rage (at his cooking, for example) and the sense of dissatisfaction he felt toward his personal intimate life—a connection that he accepted and recognized. I did not feel that I had the space to show him the connection between the narcissistic habit to repress real feelings and emotions (Lowen, 1983, 12) and the explosion of those feelings in bouts of rage. "The rage is a distorted outbreak of anger" (Lowen, 1983, 12) that bubbles up when there is no space left for them to be accepted and expressed in reality. Michael was disconnected from himself, his partner, and the new country in which he was living, and did not seem to have any emotional tool to overcome his disconnection. His volitional body was used to denying the space for real feelings to emerge and this led to a severely imbalanced life. The denial starts at first as a bodily conscious decision that then becomes, through time, a self-undermining habit. Michael seemed to be very used to denying his body the ability to feel his real emotions. Anger affects our body, it makes the muscles tense, stiffens the jaws, and reduces the depth of the breath. These bodily affections become invisible to the person who is in denial and yet they continue to operate without an actual outlet of emotions (tears of sadness) or meanings (a sense of responsibility for one's own actions). Breaking these habits and regaining real intimacy would be the real way out, but it is a challenging choice to make because it entails a complete metamorphosis.

## 1.3.2 Narcissism in Politics

Narcissism is as diffused as the damage it inflicts on the environment. Numerous studies and psychobiographies have been written concerning the life of famous political leaders affected by narcissism.[8] It is quite common that power, similar to physical appearance, becomes a way to protect the weak ego of the narcissist while irradiating its powerful image of oneself.

For example, Kernberg (1975) has described the paradox of narcissists in their professional life. Even though they reach success and status, the energies they use are in fact "pseudo-sublimatory," for the actual goal is quite exhibitionistic and directed to gain recognition, fame, and glory. The sense of entitlement to ultimate success triggers feelings of omnipotence and invulnerability at the same time. They feel that nothing can go wrong for them. Often, narcissists' professional success does not come from their skills because they do not have enough ego-strength to work with constancy on their talents, but it comes from their ability to take risks. The narcissist behaves as if "someone is watching over him, as if divine protection or charmed fate will ensure his success and well-being" (Meissner, quoted in Post, 1993a, 103). Sycophants those people around them who try to steer them away from mistakes and useless risks. As De Mause (1982) remarked, in history this dynamic is visible with Colonel House and Woodrow Wilson, Louis Howe and Franklin Delano Roosevelt, and Theodore Sorenson and John Fitzgerald Kennedy.[9]

Narcissistic leaders identify themselves with the country they lead. Using De Mause's examples, Saddam Hussein would regularly proclaim, "Saddam is Iraq and Iraq is Saddam." An Iraq without its leader, Saddam, could not have been recognized as Iraq. Similarly, Nicolae Ceausescu of Romania also demonstrated the characteristics of the malignant narcissist. Like Saddam, he created a cult of personality in the country. For both Saddam and Ceausescu, the way they demanded that their buildings be constructed was a sign of their narcissistic psychopathology: a well-fortified bunker with an escape. A pattern that is painfully recognizable in the political behavior of present and past leaders.

Another interesting point is the strong need to meet the heroic destiny of the narcissistic fantasy without which the individual would feel profoundly imbalanced. Winston Churchill, for example, felt a strong sense of accomplishment and calm when he was appointed to rule the nation in a time of intense turmoil. He was at last where he was destined to be (Kohut, 1985, 12).

Volkan (1980) has distinguished between two kinds of narcissistic leaders: "destructive charismatics," as exemplified by Hitler, and "reparative charismatics," as exemplified by Atatürk, Gandhi, and Martin Luther King, Jr. The "destructive charismatic" separates his own identity from himself and recognizes the cause of the devalued part of himself in the projections toward an external enemy. This mechanism is reflected in Hitler's scapegoating of the Jewish people, which was to become institutionalized in the destructive social policy of the Holocaust. Conversely, the "reparative charismatic" does not externalize the split but repairs it within his own nation. He "strengthens his self concept by idealizing his followers, urging them to excel, and seeing them as extensions of himself" (Volkan, 1982, 345). In both cases, there is a displacement, because a private need is rationalized and transformed into a public need but the political consequences of these two behaviors have radically different social consequences (Lasswell, 1930, 76). Similarly, Kohut (1977) has distinguished between the charismatic and the messianic personality. The charismatic personality has a fixed grandiose self but has significant elements of conscience. For the messianic personality, the self and the idealized superego are fused and there is no separate superego to constrain behaviors. Both leaders, though, can undertake decisions that are dangerous for communal resources because they are incapable of looking at the individuals that make up that community and their will since they are just a reflection of the leader's fragile ego and its projections.

### 1.3.3 Narcissism in Science

Unfortunately, scholars are not exempt from narcissistic patterns, as well. Tartakoff (1966) has coined the expression the "Nobel Prize complex" to express this endless search for acclaim by intellectually gifted narcissists (Lemaitre, 2017). Similarly to politics, the influence of narcissism on science is characterized by the need for social status and social attention. A good example of this is the story of Albert Schatz and his by then professor Selman Waksman . In 1944, Albert Schatz was mainly responsible for the discovery of the antituberculosis antibiotic streptomycin, although they both signed the first publication and the patent as he was working in Professor Waksman's laboratory. Yet, Waksman appeared to be the only discoverer as he was the only one awarded with the Nobel Prize for Medicine in 1952. Besides the difference in their social status, Waksman presented "his" discovery of streptomycin around the world suggesting an image of himself as a generous and modest benefactor of humanity. There are, of course, different versions of this story (Woodruff, 2014 and Lemaitre, 2017), yet I found meaningful what Schatz said in a later interview. He conceded to a journalist that his main surprise was that nobody had ever asked Waksman how he discovered streptomycin (Lemaitre, 2017). If true, this represents a very worrisome indicator of how the scientific community, too, seems at times more interested in form rather than in the content of a scientific discovery and is somehow disconnected from the environment in which the discovery occurs.

The other aspect of narcissism in science relates to the personal advantage that the narcissist takes in certain situations and the message that he or she spreads to others encouraging them to behave in the same way, thus costing a high amount of time and financial resources for the society to invest in creating policies capable of preventing this behavior. An example of it is the investment of a university to advertise the successes of their faculty in order to attract future investors and the attention of politicians. This effort turned some universities into a marketable commodity seemingly for sale which induced a decrease in trust.

This means that both in science and in politics, that is in the contexts where it counts the most, narcissistic traits have an important impact on the decisions we make for the goodness of the society. Since narcissistic behaviors are rewarded through an increase of power and financial means fewer policies are promoted to shape a less narcissistic inclined society. Studies show how in the US and abroad the rate of narcissism is increasing (Twenge et al., 2008; Twenge and Campbell, 2010; Wilson & Sibley, 2011) and is becoming more and more accepted as part of who we are. Consequently, the way in which the workload is collectively organized is such that an increasing number of parents will struggle to be emotionally present for their children because they are overwhelmed by their professional life. As I explained above this emotional absence increases the chances of rearing future potential narcissists (O'Boyle et al., 2012). The way in which our society is organized is such that more and more narcissists are selected for leadership positions and thus designing a community that reflects their image and needs—that is, a fragile society.[10] A Cincinnatus, a humble farmer who was twice elected political leader, willingly relinquishing power both times, and defined by Livio (1975, III, 26) as "Spes unica imperii populi romani" ("last hope for the Romans"), would never be considered as a valid leader today in certain countries. Most of our society is today fed by narcissistic traits and so speaks to our values; since narcissists act mostly in their own interest, they create a social and working environment that promotes their own unhealthy parameters (Braun et al., 2017). Hence, a narcissistic oriented society is destined to become increasingly normalized.

### 1.3.4 The Cost of Narcissism for the Environment

How much does narcissism cost the environment? As it has emerged so far, narcissism has a high impact on the community, too (Lasch, 1979). An initial cost is directly connected to the anti-systemic nature that defines narcissism as a dynamic self-regulatory system that uses the social environment in order to foster a positive self-view (Morf & Rhodewalt, 2001). Second, narcissists distort reality in order to create an environment that enhances the consideration of themselves and their value; this is evident with the grandiose fantasies that they express at work with self-inflated evaluations (e.g., Gabriel et al., 1994) and with their personal fantasy life (Raskin & Novacek, 1991). Third, they actively poison the social environment around them in order to get positive social feedback (e.g., Buss & Chiodo, 1991; Wallace & Baumeister, 2002). Moreover, they are willing to blame colleagues (Campbell et al., 2000; Gosling et al., 1998; John & Robins, 1994) or evaluators (Kernis & Sun, 1994) for faults of their own and to use disparaging attitudes when they do not receive the expected positive feedback (e.g., Bushman & Baumeister, 1998; Kernis & Sun, 1994). Fourth, their performance is not always productive especially if its purpose interferes with the goal they intend to achieve (Campbell et al., 2004; Robins & Beer, 2001). Fifth, narcissists tie their closeness to others' status and esteem, this means that they rarely act for the goodness of the collective (e.g., Campbell et al., 2000) or their family (Campbell, 1999).

### 1.3.4.1 The Tragedy of the Commons

"The tragedy of the commons" is an expression first used in an 1833 book based on several of William Foster Lloyd's lectures which became more popular a century later thanks to the work of the biologist and philosopher Hardin (1968). By tragedy of the commons, Lloyd meant all the problems raised by unregulated and shared resources, such as the atmosphere, oceans, rivers, fish stocks, roads, and highways, or even an office kitchen. People with low empathy (Batson & Moran, 1999), who are highly individualistic and whose axiological system is oriented toward consumerism would be more likely to favor the tragedy of the commons (e.g., Van Lange et al., 1997) and take more from the commons for their individual interest.

An interesting study (Campbell et al., 2005) tested this assumption and examined narcissistic behavior in relation to the tragedy of the commons dilemma. Two separate groups, the first group of narcissists and the second group of non-narcissists, were appointed to represent two different forestry companies and were asked to harvest timber from a renewable forest. The forestry company represented by the first group of narcissists harvested more timber from the very initial round. That proved that the more timber was harvested in the initial round the fastest the forest was depleted. As the study concluded, "narcissists provided a benefit to themselves but a long-term cost to other individuals and the commons" (2005, 1358). Similarly, another study (Bergman et al., 2013) noticed how narcissism is associated with lower environmental ethical values due to the higher competitive commitment to materialism. The common goods, over-fishing for example, are more likely to be exploited because individuals gloss over their belongingness to the whole.

Yet, winner of the Nobel Prize in economics, Elinor Ostrom, proposed a more optimistic view in her "Governing the Commons" (1990) and provided arguments to prove how it happens, in fact, that local communities come to access common resources and cooperate without collapse and without top-down cooperation. The story of William Kamkwamba is a good example of this communal collaboration. When he was 13 years old, he saved his village, Wimbe, in Malawi from starvation by building a wind turbine to power multiple electrical appliances to irrigate the land and make it possible to cultivate during the whole year. The village reached that tragic condition because national and international companies leveraged the desperation of the small landowners to buy and cut down the trees that were preventing the land from flooding during the rainy season. Yet, this young kid's invention and the collaboration of the people saved the village; after some initial reluctance, the people of the village trusted William's mind and combined their efforts using materials collected in a local scrapyard (blue gum trees, bicycle parts, etc.) to save the village and bring about innovation.

We do not know today how much narcissism actually costs the environment. The greediness, vanity, and thoughtlessness of certain narcissistic patterns can lead to blindness toward cogent common matters, such as climate change, wildfires, and pollution. A full-rounded bioethics should take into consideration the impact that emotional problems, such as narcissism, have on our common resources. More rigorous studies aimed at measuring the actual costs of narcissism for the environment and society are needed to realize the scale of this problem and cooperate toward viable solutions.

## Conclusion

In this chapter I discussed the problem of narcissism and its impact on the environment. The environment is, also, an important key to explaining the emotional problems involved in narcissistic patterns. In fact, the detachment from the environment generates a disengaged attitude toward those feelings, emotions, and sensations that connect the individual to a shared sense of reality. I explained why a bioethics that aims at communal survival should take into consideration the problems raised by a society in which narcissism is accepted and normalized. For this reason, I proposed an interpretation that compares narcissistic traits to a diffused health problem, like a flu. Similar to a flu, suffering often from narcissistic patterns can be draining for oneself and others as it increases the sense of loneliness and promotes carelessness toward loved ones, coworkers, and the general environment. To describe the common narcissistic patterns I used Greek and Roman mythology, specifically Ovid's interpretation of Narcissus' myth and the little known myth of Cassius and Mariam. Then, I considered the main treatments used to heal people suffering from "the narcissistic flu." This excursus served me to prepare the ground for the intentional approach I propose to use as a remedy against this flu. The most important finding emerging from the intentional approach is that real healing is possible when reconnection with the environment, the intimate one in the first place, occurs. A reconnection to the passive syntheses of their present and past life, including especially the painful memories that blocked the constitution of a safe reality, is particularly effective. This reconnection represents, in fact, the best way to reconstruct the foundation of their present life and assign real meanings and values to their lived experience. Reconnection with their present and past environment helps narcissists to fill the void left from the disruption of the intimate space caused by the lack of parental (or primary caregivers') care. Giving them the tools to look at that space and find valuable essences in there is the first step to readjust their intentional activity to a stronger ego. Finally, in the last part of the chapter I analyzed the impact that narcissism has in politics, science, and the environment with the hope that more interdisciplinary studies on this problem will follow.

## Notes

1  I discussed these problems at length in my previous book, *Human Emotions and the Origins of Bioethics* (Routledge, 2021).
2  I will use the term narcissism to refer to people with narcissistic traits, given the rarity of people affected with Narcissistic Personality Disorder (NPD). NPD is a rare character disorder that affects less than 1% of the general population (American Psychiatric Association, 1994). Moreover, NPD has been removed from the fifth edition of the Diagnostic and Statistical Manual of Mental Disorders (DSM V). As it concerns the literature around the main traits that define narcissism here are the most influential: Kets De Vries and Miller, 1985, p. 588 "Narcissists feel they must rely on themselves rather than on others for the gratification of life's needs. They live with the assumption that they cannot reliably depend on anyone's love or loyalty. They pretend to be self-sufficient, but in the depth of their beings they experience a sense of deprivation and emptiness. To cope with these feelings and, perhaps, as a cover for their insecurity, narcissists become preoccupied with establishing their adequacy, power, beauty, status, prestige, and superiority. At the same time, narcissists expect others to accept the high esteem in which they hold themselves, and to cater to their needs. What is striking in the behavior of these people is their interpersonal exploitativeness. Narcissists live under the illusion that they are entitled to be served, that their own wishes take precedence over those of others. They think that they deserve special consideration in life."; Emmons, 1987, 15: "Narcissism, rather than being a uni-dimensional construct, consists of four moderately correlated factors tapping the domains of leadership, self-admiration, superiority, and interpersonal exploitativeness. Only the Exploitativeness/Entitlement subscale was found to correlate significantly with two measures of pathological narcissism. This finding supports previous claims that this factor represents the maladaptive aspects of the trait, indicating that inter-personal maneuvers may be especially troublesome for narcissistic individuals." Maccoby, 2000, 70: "Leaders such as Jack Welch and George Soros are examples of productive narcissists. They are gifted and creative strategists who see the big picture and find meaning in the risky challenge of changing the world and leaving behind a legacy. Indeed, one reason we look to productive narcissists in times of great transition is that they have the audacity to push through the massive transformations that society periodically undertakes. Productive narcissists are not only risk takers willing to get the job done but also charmers who can convert the masses with their rhetoric. The danger is that narcissism can turn unproductive when, lacking self-knowledge and restraining anchors, narcissists become unrealistic dreamers. They nurture grand schemes and harbor the illusion that only circumstances or enemies block their success.

This tendency toward grandiosity and distrust is the Achilles' heel of narcissists. Because of it, even brilliant narcissists can come under suspicion for self-involvement, unpredictability, and—in extreme cases—paranoia." Morf and Rhodewalt, 2001, 178: "We argue that underlying narcissistic self-regulation is a grandiose, yet vulnerable self-concept. This fragility drives narcissists to seek continuous external self-affirmation. Furthermore, much of this self-construction effort takes place in the social arena. Yet, because narcissists are characteristically insensitive to others' concerns and social constraints, and often take an adversarial view of others, their self-construction attempts often misfire. Thus, although narcissistic strategic efforts generally help maintain self-esteem and affect short term, they negatively influence their inter-personal relationships and in the long run ironically undermine the self they are trying to build. The result is a chronic state of self-under-construction, which they relent-lessly pursue through various social-cognitive-affective self-regulatory mechanisms in not always optimal ways."; Rosenthal and Pittinsky, 2006, 629: "Narcissistic leadership occurs when leaders' actions are principally motivated by their own egomaniacal needs and beliefs, superseding the needs and interests of the constituents and institutions they lead. We define egomaniacal needs and beliefs to include many of the patterns per-vasive in narcissistic personality—grandiose sense of self-importance, preoccupation with fantasies of unlimited success and power, excessive need for admiration, enti-tlement, lack of empathy, envy, inferiority, and hypersensitivity (American Psychiatric Association, 2000). What is critical about this definition, and what differentiates it from simply describing narcissistic leaders, is that it is sensitive to the context in which the leadership takes place—as with theories of power motivation, narcissistic leadership considers leaders' psychological motivations; and as with charismatic leadership, nar-cissistic leadership takes situational factors and follower perceptions into account. Unlike the study of narcissistic leaders, it is not directly linked to leader personality traits, including their narcissism—non-narcissists can engage in narcissistic leadership, whereas narcissists are capable of leading non-narcissistically." Campbell et al., 2011, 269: "Narcissism is a relatively stable individual difference consisting of grandiosity, self-love and inflated self-views (For reviews see Morf & Rhodewalt, 2001; Campbell et al., 2006). It is useful to think of narcissism as containing three components: the self, interpersonal relationships and self-regulatory strategies. First, the narcissistic self is characterized by positivity, "specialness" and uniqueness, vanity, a sense of entitlement and a desire for power and esteem. Second, narcissistic relationships contain low levels of empathy and emotional intimacy. In their place, there are (often numerous) shallow relationships that can range from exciting and engaging to manipulative and ex-ploitative. Third, there are narcissistic strategies for maintaining inflated self-views. For example, narcissists seek out opportunities for attention and admiration, brag, steal credit from others, and play games in relationships. When narcissists are successful at this, they feel good—they report high self-esteem and positive life satisfaction (Sedikides et al., 2004). When they are unsuccessful, they evidence aggression and sometimes anxiety and depression (Bushman & Baumeister, 1998; Miller et al., 2007)." Pincus et al., 2014, 439: "To the layperson, narcissism is most often associated with arrogant, conceited, and domineering attitudes and behaviors, which are captured by the term narcissistic grandiosity. This accurately identifies some common expres-sions of maladaptive self-enhancement, disagreeableness, and lack of empathy asso-ciated with pathological narcissism. However, an emerging contemporary clinical model of pathological narcissism (Pincus & Lukowitsky, 2010; Roche et al., 2013) combines grandiosity with clinically important regulatory impairments that lead to self, emotional, and behavioral dysregulation in response to ego threats or self-enhancement failures."

3  Narcissistic Personality Disorder (NPD) is defined by DSM IV TR as, "a persuasive pattern of grandiosity (in fantasy or behavior), need for admiration, and lack of

empathy, beginning by early adulthood and present in a variety of contexts, as indicated by five (or more) of the following. (1) Has a grandiose sense of self-importance (e.g., exaggerates achievements and talents, expects to be recognized as superior without commensurate achievements), (2) is preoccupied with fantasies of unlimited success, power, brilliance, beauty, or ideal love, (3) believes that he or she is 'special' and unique and can only be understood by, or should associate with other special or high status people (or situations), (4) requires excessive admiration, (5) has a sense of entitlement, i.e., unreasonable expectations of especially favorable treatment or automatic compliance with his or her expectations, (6) is interpersonally exploitative, i.e., takes advantage of others to achieve his or her own ends, (7) lacks empathy: is unwilling to recognize or identify with the feelings and needs of others, (8) is often envious of others or believes that others are envious of him or her, and (9) shows arrogant, haughty behaviors or attitudes" (American Psychiatric Association, 2000, 294).

4  As it concerns the interpersonal strategies used by narcissists to keep their self inflated: they brag to keep the attention on themselves or seek for fights (Buss & Chiodo, 1991), adapt to "colorful" personae (Hogan & Hogan, 2002), associate with people in high status (Campbell, 1999), and are entertaining when they want to get something (Paulhus, 1998). These are all short term ways that logorate themselves and others in the long run (Paulhus, 1998).

5  I leave out the notion of time in this summary on purpose in order to make the argument easier to follow. Yet it needs to be reminded that time plays an important role in passive intentionality (see my *Human Emotions and the Origins of Bioethics,* chapter 2)

6  In a case study reported by McNeal (2003) George, age 48, moved away from his NPD through Ego State Therapy which consists of trance work for accessing and strengthening inner resources. In the case of George, he and his therapy accessed the realm of passive syntheses and unaware intentional acts through approaches, affect bridge technique (Watkins, 1971) for example, that required a passive state of his usual ego.

7  In this other case Michael, a 38 years old man, decides to start therapy to integrate himself in his new working environment. Although he seems to be looking for an easy fix, the therapist helps him through a deeper recovery through Kohut's approach (McLean, 2007).

8  See Houghton (2009): "Unlike other subjects addressed for the "Foundations of Political Psychology" series, narcissism does not represent a mainstream topic within the field of political psychology Current Concepts of the Narcissistic Personality: Implications for Political Psychology Author(s): Jerrold M. Post Source: Political Psychology, Vol. 14, No. 1 (Mar., 1993), pp. 99–121. Vamik Volkan, whose work is in the Kernbergian tradition, has made important clinical and theoretical contributions to the phenomenon of narcissism. See Volkan (1988, 1982) for his clinical contributions to this body of knowledge. His scholarship is particularly notable for his applications of psychoanalytic understandings of narcissism to political leaders, as exemplified by his psychobiographical study of Atatuirk (1984) and his analysis of the manner in which the need for enemies contributes to international conflict (1988). tradition, have made valuable contributions to the relationship between narcis–Charles Strozier and Marvin Zonis, both of whose work is in the Kohutian and political phenomena. An especially valuable contribution of Strozier (1983) is his application of Kohut's concept of the "group self" to leader-follower phenomena."

9  According to De Mause (1982) there are suggestions to believe that there were significant narcissistic traits in these leaders, although not enough evidence to say that they could be diagnosed with NPD.

10  See: Braun et al. (2017), 12: "Jones et al. (2004) conducted a case study analysis of a business organization operating in Australia and Southeast Asia. Data stemmed from

24 months of observation, resulting in a comprehensive journal with observation notes, personal interpretations and inferences drawn by the researcher. They were complemented with insights from semi-structured interviews with the CEO and other managerial and non-managerial staff. The authors linked the CEO's narcissistic values and behaviors (e.g., striving for affirmation, demanding obedience) to the development of a strong dominant culture. Unclear mission and goals, rewarding loyalty and commitment above performance, a rigid view of trust as the result of long tenure, and superficial happiness characterized this culture. At the same time, the authors found "a powerful counterculture comprised of professional managerial staff who hold very different values and assumptions" (Jones et al., 2004, 227) and are driven by clear achievable goals. Nevertheless, the narcissistic CEO maintains a "climate of fear, compliance and subversion of individual thought and willpower" (Jones et al., 2004, 227), creating clear distinctions between the company's in-group and out-group".

# 2

# ANXIETY

## An Emotional Geography

## Introduction

This chapter will examine how the emotional blockage generated by anxiety affects the way in which individuals experience their environment (Cloke et al., 2004) and negatively impacts their sense of safety and well-being. This discussion is divided into two parts. In the first, I will describe different types of anxiety: phobic anxiety, existential anxiety, and climate anxiety (solastalgia). In the second part, I will expound how intersubjective physical and virtual environments, such as those of a classroom and social media, can induce us to experience different forms of anxiety.

The goal for this chapter is to describe the way in which anxiety shapes the quality of an individual and intersubjective environment in order to increase the quality that our care systems can provide for those who feel unfit and unsafe in their environment (a classroom, a hospital room, a green area, etc.). Generally, the scientistic[1] assumption retains that it is up to these people to find a way to fit in, maybe through the help of psychotherapy and counseling; yet, as I will show in this chapter, I believe it is up to bioethics and the different disciplines that bioethics informs to educate us to a society capable of including these people for the promotion of communal well-being.

## 2.1 Emotional Geography

As we saw in my *Human Emotions and the Origins of Bioethics,* chapters 2 and 3, emotions affect reality (meant here as in the German *real* and *reel,* the emotional intentional content of what we feel as real and the reality in itself) and shape it according to the intensity and the relationality that they trigger. For this reason, in the 1970s, geographers specialized in human geographical research integrated emotions into their studies of human life. The turning point of emotional (Anderson & Smith 2001; Bondi 2005; Davidson and Smith 2005; Pile 2009; Smith, 2000) and affectual geography was in 2001 when Anderson and Smith proposed "a fuller programme of work, recognizing the emotions as ways of knowing, being and doing, in the broadest sense; and using this to take geographical knowledges—and the relevance that goes with them—beyond their usual visual, textual and linguistic domains" (2001, 8). From here, emotional and affectual geography developed in a multitude of interesting directions: the affectual worlds of software (Shaw & Warf, 2009; Budd & Adey, 2009), the naming of places (Bradley & Kearney, 2009), and the experience of pain (Bissell 2009).

In this chapter, I will reconstruct the emotional geography of people affected with anxiety disorders in order to describe the main constituents of reality as it appears to them and the way in which they interact with it. I will focus on how the affects that trigger the experience of intense fear can be listened to and eventually treated. Since affects represent "a transpersonal capacity which a body has to be affected (through an affection) and to affect (as the result of modifications)" (Anderson, 2006, 735; see also McCormack, 2003; Thrift, 2004) and are spatially located below cognition and consciousness and beyond reflectivity and humanness (see in my *Human Emotions and the Origins of Bioethics*, chapter 3), it is important to find channels to allow affects to express themselves without compromising one's own sense of trust toward harmonious reality in a permanent way.

### 2.1.1 The Geography of Anxiety

Emotional geography figuratively describes anxiety, in particular the anxiety of the phobic person, as a black hole. Anxiety seems to make the individuals disappear in the hole of the affects that they are experiencing without being able to actually feel. This hole sucks them into the atemporal space of everlasting affections and sensations with which they have not yet dealt. The triggering object functions as a temporal magic wand that reopens the space of the (often unknown) trauma.

In his sketch for a theory of emotions (1996/1939) Sartre showed how natural objects can become the trigger for intense fear; the anxiety that is attached to the intentional experience of an innocuous object transforms the space into a dangerous place (Davidson & Smith 2003). For example, animals that are proven to not bring particular harm to the individuals, such as lizards, can disrupt the environment of an individual. People suffering from arachnophobia describe spiders as "emotional black-holes, magically stretching and compressing the fabric of their world" (Smith et al., 2012, 61). In another example, Sartre reported the case of a young woman who was fainting at the simple sight of laurel (Sartre, 1939/1996, 50). In her case psychoanalysis helped her to recover the memory of a childhood abuse that seems to have been associated with laurel. As Fell remarked, the world as it is experienced by a phobic person is "the physical and social environment perceived as a set of attracting or repelling 'vectors' directed towards or away from various objects" (Fell, 1966, 15). For a phobic person the emotions attached to a certain object become a magic wand capable of evoking the appearance of an over-whelming, often cruel and bleak, world which Sartre described as "a world of dreams or of madness" (Sartre, 1939/1996). In this case, the phobic person is the subject of a passive intentional experience that annihilates the sense of linear time as one normally experiences it and brings him/her back to the spatiotemporal point in which that trauma took place. Yet, only the emotional and affective valence of that experience is present, the cognitive representation of it has yet to be brought to the surface. Transforming that experience from a passive into an active one requires the commitment to a healing process that I will examine later in the chapter.

Geographers working in the phenomenological tradition claimed that any thorough existential presentation of the geographical life-world "must also recognize and examine the personal and cultural dimensions of a particular environmental and placed experience" (Seamon & Sowers, 2009). The arc described by affects, sensations, and then emotions, which shows the trajectory of passive intentionality, gives meaning to the world of experience in such a way that "the emotional subject and the object of the emotions are unified in an indissoluble synthesis" (Sartre, 1996/1933). As far as this synthesis remains on a passive level the subject has no tools to free him/herself from the bleakness evoked by those emotions. The reality of a person external to those emotions can help to smoothen the emotional turmoil triggered by the object; an example from an actual lived-experience would be:

> Our boiler is in the cellar, and the pilot light keeps going out, so I stay here and freeze all day because I won't go and light the pilot light until my husband gets home, which is ridiculous. But I won't go.
>
> *(Zara, cited in Smith et al., 2012, 67)*

Just the existence of the object has the power to compromise the reality of the phobic person; yet, the reality of a person who is familiar to them has the strength to fight back the threats that the phobic reality announces with its dreadful objects:

> Sort of unconsciously I do it, check that there's no spiders on the towels or you know before I have a bath because I've been caught out that way. [...] in people's houses, I just, before I shut the door, you know, I'm looking all around to make sure that there's no spider
>
> *(Zara cited in Smith et al., 2012, 67)*

I cannot fall asleep peacefully without having visions of lizards (Carla, my client, 2019)

Emotions have a life of their own that meets (for some subjects only occasionally) one's personal life. They are our environment but as we saw in my *Human Emotions and the Origins of Bioethics,* chapter 3, they have their own intentionality that is driven by sensations and affections. The environment is part of us and we are part of the environment; we cannot choose when an emotion (instantiation of an environmental meaning) will arise and how long it will last. As Sartre wrote, "One cannot get out of <the emotion> as one pleases, it fades away of itself, but one cannot put a stop to it. [...] If we are really to be seized by horror we have not only to mime it, we must be spell-bound and filled to overflowing by our own emotion." (1996 [1939], 75–76). An emotion is as concrete as the bricks that make the walls that are in front of me. I cannot get out of a daunting emotion unless I commit to its concreteness and start looking for the door. "The linear time and geographical space that separates the phobic person from its trigger object collapses because of the emotional reaction, the categories of the world act immediately upon the consciousness, they are present to it at no distance" (Sartre, 1996 [1939], 90). When the affects elicit a phobic reaction the geographical distance that separates the person from the phobic object disappears because the person disappears. The phobic object takes all the space that is left because the timeless temporality of the emotions takes over the linear time of the individual. So, the rules and categories of the world as we know them disappear.

> The window pane, which would have to be broken, the distance which would have to be traversed in order for the grinning man to attack me, are obscured. All rules are suspended. I tremble as if I were being directly attacked.
>
> *(client cited in Fell, 1966, 29)*

The phobic object whose emotional charge is different from the object itself contaminates and pollutes the reality of the person affected by this fear (Douglas, 1993); it represents something both disgusting and abject (Kristeva, 1982; Sibley, 1995). As Sartre remarked:

> The phobic cannot help obsessively exercising this (literally) self-defeating dialectic with real and unreal intentional objects, despite the psychic damage her imaginative actions cause: the tragic nature of the obsession is derived from the fact that the mind forces itself to reproduce the object of which it stands in fear [...] the obsession is willed, reproduced by a sort of dizziness, by a spasm of spontaneity.
>
> *(1983 [1940], 14)*

The affects that animate the obsession are stronger than the will of the individual. That is the core tragedy of an obsession, which is often triggered by the unwillingness of the individual to deal with their own feelings and sensations at the time in which they arise. Hence, these sensations found their own voice in the obsession. The "magic black hole" into which the phobic person falls every time the fears take over is the pre-reflective and passive space of affections and sensations. When the hole is avoided the phobic person still knows that the threatening space is there as a vile presence into which all her life could be sucked and disappear. It is true that the black hole is still there because work needs to be done to address those affections and transform their intimidating presence into vitality. The work that needs to be done to heal the overwhelming fear is to transform the surrounding space of the phobic person into an amicable one and restore trust into the harmoniousness of life. For this reason, it is necessary to bring pre-reflection into reflection (see my *Human Emotions and the Origins of Bioethics,* chapter 3) and transform affections into emotions and meanings. Primal sensations trigger scary emotions that can, in this way, express their intentionality. Yet, this expression can harm the organic balance of the individuals if they do not confront those affections and understand the actual threat that they constitute in daily life. An example that I will discuss later in this chapter (in section 1.3.2) would be to have a phobic attack at the sight of a lizard running close to your foot and, after the event, avoiding thinking about it.

### 2.1.2 Existential versus Phobic Anxiety

Existential and phobic anxiety can trigger similar forms of panicking reactions; yet, existential anxiety cannot be treated and healed in the same way as the phobic form. As existential philosophers and psychotherapists have remarked anxiety as the awareness of our own mortality is a fact that we need to accept and make part of our daily lives. Tillich, for example, wrote:

> The description of anxiety as the awareness of one's finitude is sometimes criticized as untrue from the point of view of the ordinary state of mind. Anxiety, one says, appears under special conditions but is not an ever-present implication of the human's finitude. Certainly anxiety as an acute experience appears under definite conditions. But the underlying structure of finite life is the universal condition which makes the appearance of anxiety under special conditions possible. Two of the threats to my existence are the threats of the loss of time and the loss of space. Life is temporary, and the space that belongs to me may be gone at any time. For example, when I think about running late to a movie that I have looked forward to seeing, I notice that I say, "I am 'anxious' to get there." Or, when I think about losing my place in line after waiting for 20 minutes to get to the cash register, I realize that I get frustrated and angry. (1952b, 20)

Losing space and losing time are the triggers for both existential anxiety and phobic anxiety, but in this case they refer to an undeniable intersubjective human reality. We feel anxious because it is true that we will disappear in time and space; that is a fact of our humanness. These triggers, concretely, point to the disappearance of our being, while phobic anxiety focuses on the threats that might damage our integrity. While existential anxiety is an underlying condition to being human, phobic anxiety represents the occasional threat with which we have not yet dealt with and it comes back to bother us in our daily lives. Phobic anxiety can shutter our being into pieces while we are still sitting there looking at our own disintegration from the darkness of our hole; existential anxiety is a concrete promise that our being will be shattered eventually.

In the case of existential anxiety, the ontological facticity of the anxiety generated by the awareness of our transient statute should give us the courage to live the time and space we have as meaningfully as possible. From the standpoint of existential philosophy and psychology, anxiety is "a natural, multifaceted response to both the freedom and the responsibility associated with making daily choices about how to live one's life" (Roemer et al., 2009). While existential anxiety invites appreciation of life, phobic anxiety invites the resolution of unquestioned affections underlying the unity of our being.

## 2.1.3 Solastalgia: A Form of Climatic Existential Anxiety

Solastalgia is a neologism coined by the philosopher Albrecht (2005)[2] to indicate the sense of anxiety that derives from the climatic impact on the environment. The term was introduced for the first time in 2003 at an Ecohealth Forum in Montreal. This word expresses the lost sense of comfort (in Latin, *solacium*) combined with the consequent growing distress (from Greek, *algos*—ἄλγος) that arises from seeing one's own space changing because of climatic problems. Different from homesickness, solastalgia is a form of anxiety directed toward a place that actually still exists but disappeared while the individual was still inhabiting it (something very similar to what occurred with the covid-19 pandemic). This state of anxiety originates, in fact, from a very complex notion of place (Galway et al., 2019).

### 2.1.3.1 Lockdown and Solastalgia

Jean-Luc Nancy describes the notion of place as the space of community or being with the Other as an opening of being to itself as a common space (1993, p. 78). I think it is this notion of place that came to collapse during the lockdown caused by the covid-19 pandemic, wildfires, and other natural disasters (that climate change is presenting more and more often to our lives). The collapse of the familiar places, such as the workplace, the playground, the gym, or a church, lead to a loss of sense of belongingness and consequent contamination of the inner space to the outer space. The inner space expanded outside. This means that the emotional space of interiority became the space where to encounter ourselves and the Other without any chance for real alterity to be generated. In each part of this newly contained space we encounter first ourselves with no possibility to escape.

During these months of lockdown we had to learn a new way of interpreting our place. Suddenly, we found ourselves confined to our home, the spaces to which we used to belong collapsed and took with itself a piece of our identity. We stopped being students, professionals, friends; we stopped getting dressed to go to work, feeling touched by the ones we love, finding shelter in a classroom away from problematic parents; all these forms of spatial alterity that used to shape us in the same way as a glass gives shape to water, disappeared leaving us with our inner world becoming larger and larger. There was, of course, the space to gather these identities within ourselves but it required a new effort that felt unnatural. The space of natural belongingness that was naturally paced by our society has disappeared and we had to learn how to tame our inner space so that it would not take all the space left empty from the disappearance of outer places. Learn how to co-live with our loved ones, how to work with our colleagues from home, how to keep in touch with our friends without hanging out outside. During and immediately after the lockdown, solastalgia has been aggravated by the contraction of *Spielraum* or *jeu*, leeway (Merleau-Ponty, 2012) generated by the obligation of wearing masks outside and when in potential contact with other people. The event—literally *venire, e* something that happens to me out of nothing—of the lockdown "rob me of individuality and freedom" (Merleau-Ponty, 2012, 290). The space of our lived-experience became so contracted that we could literally no longer breathe (2012, 299). The reduction of breath induced by wearing masks represented another way to conflate the intimate with the outer space. Once again, the alterity of space that allows my inner emotional reality to be other than mine collapsed and inevitably produced anxiety, inertia, and physical discomfort.

## 2.1.3.2 The Questions to Address

Albrecht's groundbreaking paper (2005) described cases of both acute and chronic space degradation in which solastalgia arose: persistent drought in rural New South Wales and the mining communities in the Upper Hunter Valley. Both environments became unwelcoming for the communities that were still living there because of dramatic climatic environmental changes and poor management of natural resources. This transformation generated a sense of loss and powerlessness for the individuals belonging to those communities; the environment on which their vital and emotional survival depended was so endangered that the individuals were left with a sense of personal deprivation and failure (Tschakert & Tutu, 2010). These are the words that Albrecht and colleagues used to define this lived-experience:

It is the pain experienced when there is recognition that the place where one resides and that one loves is under immediate assault (physical desolation). It is manifest in an attack on one's sense of place, in the erosion of the sense of belonging (identity) to a particular place and a feeling of distress (psychological desolation) about its transformation. It is an intense desire for the place where one is a resident to be maintained in a state that continues to give comfort or solace. Solastalgia is not about looking back to some golden past, nor is it about seeking another place as "home." It is the "lived experience" of the loss of the present as manifested in a feeling of dislocation; of being undermined by forces that destroy the potential for solace to be derived from the present. In short, solastalgia is a form of homesickness one gets when one is still at "home."

*(2005, 42)*

As this passage shows with clarity, "place" is, here, a key term to understand the quality of suffering provoked by solastalgia. The place, which was considered essential for the emotional and physical survival of the individual and their community, is endangered. The place of the solstagic person is the familiar environment as it used to be before the occurrence of the dramatic changes produced by natural and climatic disasters. According to Trujillo (2009) place here does not indicate any ordinary space; the space is not a landscape to enjoy but the structure that holds together the lives of all those belonging to that space. Without this structure these lives will feel empty and amorphous. As Trujillo wrote, "where the colonizers [and by extension mining, agribusinesses, oil and lumber interests [...] saw a space-landscape, natives saw a place" (2009, 12).

A variety of factors can trigger this condition: extreme weather events, such as flooding, drought, or earthquakes (e.g., Warsini et al., 2014), resource extraction (e.g., Canu et al., 2017), climate change (e.g., Tschekart et al., 2013), and political violence (e.g., Sousa et al., 2014). These transformative factors can be distinguished into acute and chronic. Acute triggering factors can be floods, wildfires, or earthquakes that abruptly transform the environment into a desolate place without its community having time to adjust to it; while the chronic factors involve a gradual degradation of places such as sea level rise or drought. Climate change leads to both acute impacts (e.g., floods and wildfires) and chronic degradation of places (e.g., sea level rise); the words that are commonly being used "to describe these changes on the environment are: 'cumulative,' 'compounding,' 'imposed,' 'unwelcome,' 'unwanted,' 'dramatic,' 'negative,' and 'profound/ intense'" (Galway et al., 2019, online; Albrecht, 2005; 2010; Pannel, 2018).

Given the reality of the fast pace at which our climate is changing,[3] this form of anxiety might afflict a larger and larger number of people thus generating growing distress and a new range of mental, emotional, and spiritual health problems. It is already observable how the global suicide rates have increased by 50% in the last 50 years and rates of mental illness or psychological and psychiatric disorders have also increased (WHO, 2014). In Asia, for example, psychiatrists have shown the interconnection between rising temperature and suicides. A 2013 meta-analysis of 60 studies concluded that every standard deviation of warming in global temperatures corresponded to a 4% rise in interpersonal violence and a 14% rise in intergroup conflict (Kim, 2013). In 2015, the Lancet Commission on Health and Climate Change recognized solastalgia as a key dimension for understanding global mental health and its changes through climatic impact.

The questions that are important for bioethics and environmental ethics to address given the situation are: "how can individuals and groups cope with solastalgic distress? Can the restoration of degraded landscapes help people to cope with distress and enable healing? Can interventions focused on collective healing enable coping with solastalgia in ways that promote human and ecosystem health?" (Pannell, 2018)

### 2.1.4 Approaches to Emotional Dysregulation

According to the WHO's 2017 report, 260 million people suffer from anxiety disorders worldwide; in the United States anxiety disorders are the most common problems in mental health (Narrow et al., 2002).[4] I believe that these problems are still afflicting our society so strongly because for a long time emotions have been discarded as inappropriate disruptions and their main cure was considered to be suppression. Science is still struggling to pay due attention to emotions and give them their dignity as a proper subject of study.

In psychology, emotional disorders have been often connected to cognition and treated as cognitive problems, hence moving the focus from emotions to cognition. Anxiety disorders are considered to be a disturbance in information processing that consequently leads to over- or underestimation of the danger of the perceived threat (Beck et al., 1985). This cognitive way of interpreting the disturbance is often associated with the person's belief of one's own inability to succeed when facing the threat. As Clark (1986, 1988, 1996) remarked, catastrophic misinterpretations of somatic sensations are more likely to generate panic disorders in the future (Clark & Wells, 1995). Early theories on the development and treatment of anxiety disorders generally suggested that fear develops through traumatic conditioning (e.g., Marks, 1969; Wolpe, 1958) and is maintained operantly through avoidance learning (Mowrer, 1947). For this reason, anxiety has been defined as irrational cognition (Bouton et al., 2001).

Understanding how emotions affect anxiety is unfortunately a relatively new approach to the problem (Greenberg & Safran, 1987).[5] Skinner, for example, moved the causal role that emotions hold in human behaviors to conditioning. Similarly, classical cognitive therapy considered emotions only a byproduct of cognition (e.g., Beck et al., 1985) and an outcome of the epistemological life of the individual. On the other hand, as I showed in my *Human Emotions and the Origins of Bioethics,* chapters 1 through 3, I believe that emotions need to be considered independently of cognition as they are as important as cognitions and often influence the genetic constitution of cognitions.

Yet, Thompson (1990) stressed that emotions need to be restrained and under control throughout all human life; their arousal should be diminished as much as possible in public and private places (see expression of anger, for example). Emotional hyper- and hyporeactivity (Berenbaum et al., 2003) have to be regulated either through control or suppression of the emotional experience. This belief is restated in emotion theory, too (see Ekman & Davidson, 1994) where emotions are defined as "disruptive entities that impede functioning and success" (Frijda, 1986) and respond to the environment in an adaptive and goal-oriented way (Frijda, 1986). For this reason, they believe that highly emotional instability of the human being (Efran et al., 1990) is inevitable and will accompany them their whole life.

A less resigned model of emotional regulation has been proposed (Mennin et al., 2002; 43) and considers emotional disruption caused by anxiety as "1. heightened intensity of emotions; 2. poor understanding of emotions; 3. negative reactivity to one's emotional state (e.g., fear of emotion); and 4. maladaptive emotional management responses." Differently, from previous, more repressive models, this approach tries to read emotions according to their inner autonomous structure and in relation to the impact that they have on the individual. In particular, Barlow (2002) has described anxiety and mood disorders as emotional dysfunctions of the way in which one is used to process emotions—hence, they do not need to be repressed but only properly listened to and processed. The hierarchical structure of anxiety and mood pathology (Clark and Watson (1991), Brown et al. (1998), and Zinbarg and Barlow, 1996) have shown how negative affects negatively impact the symptomatology of moods and anxiety. This leads analytic theorists to reintroduce emotions in the etiology of anxiety disorder despite the complexity that each emotion involves. Moreover, Friman et al. (1998) have argued that anxiety and emotions, in general, as concepts should not be avoided by radical behaviors. Emotions, even those that bring us pain, are an important cue to understand one's own sense of reality.

## 2.1.4.1 Treating Phobias through Intentional Acceptance

Cognitive Behavioral Therapy proposed to treat phobias through high exposure techniques with the goal to overcome anxiety by modifying the behavioral answer of the client to the potential threat. By gradually exposing the client to the object that triggers the phobic reaction the person learns how to cope with catastrophizing and negative thoughts and transform them into a helpful way of thinking. Moreover, it educates the client to recognize the physical reaction that accompanies the phobic event and exert a constructive way of thinking how to keep the bodily sensations under control. This helps the person to learn that they are capable of surviving after being in contact with the trigger of their fears and anxiety. It is proved, though, that even if very effective exposure therapy does not necessarily achieve long-lasting effects (Booth & Rachman, 1992; Craske et al., 1995; Fava et al., 1994; Foa & Jaycox, 1999; Gould et al., 1997; Lovell et al., 2001; Marks et al., 1998; Tarrier et al., 1999). For this reason, Hayes (2005) proposed new forms of cognitive therapy: acceptance and commitment therapy (ACT; Hayes et al., 1999) and mindfulness based cognitive therapy (MBCT; Segal et al., 2002) that build on traditional cognitive and behavioral approaches but with an emphasis on the acceptance of one's own emotions and their inability to change them.

Orsillo (Orsillo et al., 2003; Roemer & Orsillo, 2005; Roemer et al., 2006) described acceptance-based behavioral therapy as the approach that acknowledges

> The importance of accepting or allowing the presence of internal experiences (as an alternative response to the judgmental and avoidant reactions to these experiences that are characteristic of individuals with anxiety and other disorders) while developing behavioral repertoires that are broad, flexible, effective, and values driven (to counteract the rigid, restricted, and avoidant behavioral patterns that are typical of individuals with anxiety disorders).
>
> *(Orsilio et al., 2013, 24).*

Since it is clear that deliberate efforts to control and suppress negative emotions increase the effect of the distress in certain contexts (e.g., Gross & Levenson, 1997; Purdon et al., 1999; Roemer & Borkovec, 1994; Wegner, 1994), the acceptance-based approach is focused on expanding the client's awareness of his or her experience and encourages a shift in response to internal reactions.

I believe that this technique has more chances to help the phobic person than the sole cognitive behavioral approach; compassionate acceptance of the painful experience is, in fact, a very (if not the most) efficient way to restore intimacy with one's own pre-reflective disorganized emotions and affections. Since the final goal is to increase one's quality of life, learning to live with the chronic distress of an anxiety disorder is more convenient than self-blaming, feeling inadequate, and being overly self-doubting. The overall goal is to encourage the client to engage in behaviors that aim to change negative thoughts and feelings, but also to reduce the internal struggle that they might create and generate meanings out of it. The key element is the allowance of their rise and passage without attempts to avoid or control this experience (Segal et al., 2002).

In this sense, I think that being able to engage with one's own passive, practical, and active intentionality (see in my *Human Emotions and the Origins of Bioethics,* chapter 3 and the next two sections) can help to increase the client's acceptance of their own lived experience as well as expand the meaning of its own reality. Focusing on the transition from passive to practical intentionality, in which the client becomes the subject observer of its own affects and lower feelings, can ignite a compassionate outlook toward their own suffering or dysregulation. It is possible to strengthen the perceptual and emotional understanding of one's own lower feelings (passive intentionality) by transforming each step of the exposure experience into meanings that bring value to its own life (active intentionality)

## 2.1.4.2 Laura, a Case Study

When I knew Laura, she was a graceful, cheerful 24-year-old woman who had suffered from a fear of lizards (herpetophobia) since she was a toddler. At the time I met her, she was studying film in New York and wanted to make a documentary for her school about her phobia. For this reason, she asked me to meet with her and a close friend who would have filmed our sessions. Initially I accepted but then I had second thoughts. I realized that her friend, the camera, and her project could be an impediment to her healing as they might actually have been part of her problem. She admitted more than once in our introductory conversation that she used her network of trustworthy friends and colleagues as a shield to cope with her anxiety. She had developed a way to use the people around her as a means to grapple with her fears without having to deal with them directly.

With her insistence, and despite my reservations, we kept the camera and decided to meet for three days in a row as she was only visiting the city for a short time. She had already tried exposure therapy and hypnosis and said that her anxiety had been better ever since, but now she wanted to be completely free from the phobia. Once again, she seemed to delegate the responsibility for her healing to an external agent—therapy. When the effects of her phobia were at their worst, she was living in a very distressing period of her life. At that time, she had to go back to a school she did not like and was recovering from the betrayal of a close friend who had shared sensitive information about her life with others. She felt alone and vulnerable, was diagnosed with depression, and was encouraged to take light medications to deal with it. Her therapist, the constant presence of her boyfriend, and the coming of the summer helped her to overcome her depression without the use of the medications. Talking with me about it a few years later, she associated her depression with the university and not to her phobia.

When asked, she could not remember what first triggered her phobia. She recalled that at five she became scared of lizards when one quickly jumped on her while she was playing in the garden. By the time of our meeting, she was mostly scared if lizards were at face level, so much so that she could not drive the car into her garage at home but always asked her father to do it. She admitted that the birth of her twin brothers when she was five might have been one of the reasons her phobia developed. She was trying to attract the attention of her parents—she did not seem so convinced of that hypothesis, although she was the one who brought it up (maybe the intervention of the previous therapist contributed to it). She considered her phobia still very disruptive in her life. She wanted to go hiking or visit exotic places, but she was incapable due to the fear she nurtured toward open spaces.

To help her I prepared a questionnaire based on a mix of CBT, intentional meditation, and acceptance-based approaches (Appendix A). She seemed very eager to start exposure therapy but was not particularly enthusiastic about the questionnaire. From the questionnaire it emerged that she had very little, if any, compassion toward herself for what she was going through. When I warned her that her phobia might keep coming and going throughout her life, she seemed disappointed, yet she looked more accepting when I proposed to her a comparison with a diabetic person. I told her that she could have a good quality of life, but she needed to take care of her emotional problems every now and then. Parenthetically, I noticed that emotions are often seen by clients as a caprice of their bodies rather than important qualities of which they need to take care of. Some precautions about avoidance and exposure time needed to be taken into consideration and transformed into good habits to apply systematically in her daily life. It emerged, in fact, from the questionnaire that she hardly ever exposed herself to lizards, never challenged her phobia, and, when she put herself in a situation that she would consider of high anxiety, she always used someone else to shield herself from the threat. In the exploratory phase of our work I proposed to her some exercises for her to work on alone, but she seemed very unhappy about them, though during our time together she became more and more open to them.

After our first day working together, my understanding was that she had not yet had an intimate conversation with herself about her phobia. The attempts she made to focus on her phobia were always defeated by a very judgmental internal voice, never compassionate or comforting. She blamed herself for giving in to something as irrational and risible as her lizard phobia. While practicing meditation and breathing exercises with her, I asked what images were connected to the thoughts she had about herself and her phobias. She answered that she saw herself much smaller than anything else. Because of this, I made it my goal to help her reach a more comfortable perceptual size, to make contact with her strengths, and, hopefully, to put her in a more compassionate position towards herself. To this end, I introduced her to intentional meditative practice, that is, a meditative practice whose goal is to reconnect with the intentional network that bridges together the "two leaves" of our being, the reflective and the ontological one, (Merleau-Ponty, 2012) to ourselves and our environment. Ideally, in intentional meditative practice the individual experiences the lower feelings of the organic body (uneasiness of the chest, tensions in the stomach, heavy legs, and so on). If listened to, these feelings evoke higher feelings and their intentional trajectory; for example, experiencing uneasiness while breathing might evoke a sense of sadness or could be a symptom of repressed intense fear (Dowling, 2018). At the end of the meditation, when these sensations are actively observed, examined, and transformed from the client into feelings (a common misunderstanding is that feelings are spontaneous, but it is not so. The transformation of sensations into feelings can be quite problematic), we proceed to understand the active intentional level prompted by this meditative state. The questions that can be raised at this level are: what are the meanings you assign to these feelings? What thoughts do they evoke? What kind of values are implied in these thoughts? These questions help to describe the client's intentional arc, that is their passive intentionality (sensations, lower and higher feelings), practical intentionality (becoming aware of those feelings), and active intentionality (assigning meanings and values to those feelings).

At the very beginning, Laura's response to bodily feelings was quite low and not very descriptive. It was as if she could not make contact with where her body was and that showed in her appearance, as well. As Peirce wrote: "feeling is not equivalent to consciousness, rather it is an element of consciousness" (cited in Ferrarello, 2019). The fact that we have feelings does not mean that we know how to feel those feelings. Often feelings remain at the level of sensations. Laura seemed to have difficulty in feeling her feelings. Her appearance, too, revealed a cognitive predominance of her character. She was very thin, and everything in her look was carefully studied and chosen according to the way in which it should have appeared to others. On the other hand, her best friend, who came with her in order to film the documentary, looked completely different from her and emanated a sense of earthly strength. I wondered if that earthly strength was the physical quality Laura was unconsciously looking for in the people she chose to have around her, those who could protect her from the physical threats of life. During our first encounter, Laura stayed on the level of higher feelings (fear, anger, etc.). Generally, this means that the person does not feel her own sensations but feels the expectations imposed on her feelings by herself and others. This makes the reconnection with the body a little harder because it skips immediately to the active level (the level of meanings and values assignation) without building any solid grounding in the flesh. This type of connection is, generally, not sustainable in the long run and is heavily influenced by outside validations.

With time, her description of the intentional arc improved, and she was able to provide very detailed and useful descriptions of her bodily sensations and the feelings associated with them. That allowed her to recognize the bodily feelings preceding a phobic attack and eventually to reassure herself that these sensations would not invalidate her or make her small and powerless. She described how during the phobic episode her breath used to come up and stop in her lower chest. At that point, she felt warmth on her skin, the mind would go blank, and the stomach opened up as if something was making its way out from inside her and would eventually take over. This description was incredibly vivid. I followed up on it with some questions through which she expounded in more detail how it would feel like this "something" would crawl up through her body and eventually she was no longer herself. She would go blank, lose control over everything, and witness what was happening to herself from a distance. "As if you abandon yourself?" I asked. "Exactly," she answered, "it feels like a betrayal."

In our second meeting we prepared for the exposure encounter using intentionality meditation and dialogic exercises. I needed to know to what extent she was willing to expose herself to the very source of her anxiety, how much she knew about lizards and how her bodily sensations, feelings, and thoughts would react to an encounter with lizards; also, I investigated her coping and avoidance strategies. At the end of this work, we compiled together an exposure hierarchy list that felt challenging yet safe for her. We created, also, practical exercises that she could practice by herself monthly in order to reinforce both the results of the exposure encounter and her independence in relation to the source of her anxiety. This conversation was accompanied step by step by intentional meditation aimed at reconnecting with the passive and active layers of the body. It was important for me to make sure that she was fully grounded in her body and her thoughts were not just hetero-directed. If her mind was fully aligned with her body then it would be possible to access her intimate space and, hopefully, reconnect her with the part of herself that felt abandoned and judged.

For this reason, I invited her to describe again the sensations she was feeling at that moment and to compare them with the sensations she has when she imagines the source of her anxiety being close to her. This description was quite similar to the one she provided the day before: racing heart, shortness of breath, sweating, and solar plexus contractions (the day before she indicated it as stomach but maybe all the three areas, chest, stomach, and solar plexus, were involved). She described that feeling as if the world would collapse on her through the solar plexus. When I asked her to elaborate on the sense of unreality that she felt during a phobic episode the answer became more elaborate and in depth. "My world is like a circle (she used the meditation setting I provided her with in our previous meeting since she found it reassuring and helpful) and it is wide but then the lizard is there and it collapses. Everything fades away and it is just me and her."

This description resonates with the description of the black hole I presented earlier. I decided to stop for a moment and challenge her description. I remember that in more than one instance she described the trusted people in her life as a shield. I found this statement very worrisome and potentially the source of her resistance to overcoming the phobia because it indicated her difficulty establishing a real intimate bond with herself and her own body. For this reason, I asked her if the others would disappear as well. She told me that the others do not disappear if they are engaged in actively protecting her. This dynamic made me think of a strong split that took place between herself and her body. A deep part of her body did not trust her anymore, so she had to delegate her safety to an external source. She judged herself incompetent to take care of herself. Clearly, this resulted in a very deep form of distress and emotional pain. Going off this, I asked her if there were objects or parts of her body that could function as a shield to prevent the world from disappearing, to keep her anchored to reality when she felt vulnerable. So, we agreed to try using a clenching-fist move to protect herself in the future. During the meditation exercises, I also encouraged her to thank herself for the care she was dedicating to herself and the protection she was offering to herself in order to reach an acceptable state of well-being. All these exercises were focused on creating a comfortable intimate space that would have prepared her for the exposure encounter.

On the active cognitive level of the intention, we explored together how much she knew about the basic facts concerning lizards' biology, how they see, their sense of sociality, and their potential threat. The goal was to explore the implied meanings relating to her encounters with lizards and to generate from there more fitting meanings to that reality. We proceeded in these exercises through epoché (more on this term in my *Human Emotions and the Origins of Bioethics*, chapter 3), which means that we tried as much as possible to suspend any moral and cognitive assumptions and judgments. Statements such as: "You should feel ashamed of thinking that..." or "you should not feel that since..." were suspended, although they kept coming up and disturbing the thinking process. While keeping in mind the threats that lizards would constitute for her, I invited her to challenge her fears and to try to think of ways in which she could feel safe if she found herself alone with lizards. At the end of the process, we gathered together five strategies that would have helped her to cope with her anxiety by herself, two of which were meditative and the other three practical.

1.  Fist clenching: as an immediate meditative transfer to a happy and safe place.
2.  Water pistols: to keep in her bag in case lizards came close.
3.  Protecting circles: as a meditative way to see herself as separated from lizards.
4.  Body Movements: to signal lizards that she is there and the need for them to stay distant from her.
5.  Team-up with the body as a way to reassure the body that she is going to be there for it.

It was the fifth strategy, in particular, that she found important and resonated with her needs. She appreciated the idea of "making peace" with her body and to reassure it that she would be there for it. I reinforced this point by the intentional meditative practice in which I guided her to open a conversation with her body and, where possible, to promise that she would be there for it. Besides this, I asked her to acknowledge if she felt gratitude about the work she did up to that point and to express it in some sentences or gestures.

It was when I asked her to make a list of her avoidance and coping strategies that I saw a slight emotional shift in her. I stopped and asked how she was feeling. At that moment, she dropped the judgmental armor about her state and said that she was feeling very sorry for herself and for how small her world had become because of her phobia. She felt that she forced herself to live in a shell and she did not like that. She wanted to overcome that feeling. Through the list we compiled together it became evident that she could not lead a normal life by herself because any chance to encounter the phobic object would have disrupted her world and her forced sense of reality. Her daily life was meticulously calculated based on shielding herself from the potential encounter; most of her life could have a normal pace because of the vicarious help of her trusted people. It is worth noticing that at the time we met the client had chosen to live in New York although her parents used to live in Switzerland, the country where we had our sessions. Her life as a child and adolescent had been surrounded by potential encounters while her chosen life as a grownup was going to be in a city that would have helped her to finally avoid lizards and conduct a more normal life. She said that this choice came to her on an unconscious level.

In order to bring her avoidant mechanisms to the surface we wrote a list of possible encounters from least scary to most in order to help her to acknowledge the likelihood of her survival in case an encounter had occurred. Different from a cognitive behavioral approach, this list was organized after a meditative approach with which I invited Laura to reconnect with her body and environment. At the end of the day, when the list was ready, we agreed on meeting the next day close to a forest with which I am very familiar. The goal was to let her take a walk in the forest under the September sun on a gravel ground where encounters with lizards would have been very likely. I asked her to focus on her enjoyment despite the high probability of encountering a lizard. It was important to take a walk by herself and to try to register the feelings with which her body was responding to that environment. How does the resistance of the gravel feel on your feet? How does it feel for you to smell the fresh grass? Do you enjoy the sound of the leaves moved by the breeze on the trees? In case a state of anxiety would have arisen, I was ready to come where she was and to help her.

The walk went very well. She did not feel the need to ask for help. She told me that she realized how much she missed being in nature and walking by herself in the greenery. She went into the woods afraid but came out a champion. Unfortunately, she did not meet any lizards, but she was open to another suggestion of mine, that is to go to an animal shop and ask the shop assistant to touch one.

Yet, I knew that there was still more work to be done, when we walked back to my office, in fact, I noticed that she disappeared. Her body was still there, of course, but she was using me as a shield and her level of attention toward the shared intersubjective space in which we were both living was much smaller. It was as if she was not there for me in the same way she used to be. She was using me for her survival. Once in the office I challenged this behavior and we worked on all this information. Of course, she did not want to be unavailable for others and herself when she was in open green areas; she wanted to enjoy the outside reality in a spontaneous way without the need to program her reactions. To this goal we did intentional meditative exercises and I prescribed her a, figuratively speaking, diet to take every two months consisting of going out in a green area for 30 minutes and focusing on enjoying the space and being in it without using others as a shield. The goal of this exercise was to transform her intentional active behavior in passive intentionality and, thus, in unconscious habit. This transformation would have allowed her to live the natural life in a more spontaneous way because she would have strengthened the bond with her body and acknowledged the efforts she had made to overcome her anxiety.

On the day of our last meeting, Laura told me she had gained much more confidence in herself. In particular, she appreciated the meditative scenarios and the awareness that came to her from reconnecting with her body, which she imagined as her two hands closed in a shake, and helped her to feel secure. This sense of self-confidence, she told me, was proved by the fact that she had faced, by herself, one of her worst-case scenario encounters without giving in to panic. The night before our last meeting, she found a lizard right on top of the key holder of her home. This same situation had happened to her half a year ago, as well. The first time, the scene terrified her so much that she panicked and called her boyfriend for help. But the night before our meeting, Laura found the courage to face the lizard and get the key to the house. Moreover, during our last session I created some of the scenarios she mostly feared, for example sitting outside with her feet down to the floor or walking alone in the woods and in an open field, and she managed to face these scenarios by herself without panicking or putting in practice an avoidance mechanism. Each scenario was prepared and followed by intentional meditation so that she could be close and perceptive of her bodily feeling. Each exercise was followed up by a short debriefing of her thoughts and feelings.

She left my office feeling stronger, more willing to face her fears, and capable of feeling compassionate toward them without using others as a shield. She felt that she could rely on her self-strength—she affirmed. She seemed to be willing to try new experiences like feeding a lizard or sunbathing in a place where there are potentially several lizards. Weeks later, I received an email from her in which she told me about the new experiences she was able to face without feeling stressed or having people around her.

## 2.1.4.3 Intentionality: A Commentary

Focusing on one's own intentional activity is an effective way to educate the client to handle their own emotions while paying attention to the shape they give to their reality. Different from mindfulness, this practice focuses on the description of the entire intentional arc from passive actions to willing decisions. The ultimate goal, in fact, is to create a disinterested compassionate witness to one's own reality, as if the self would appear to the witness as an intentional object itself. This witness should gradually be able to embrace the clients' fears and restore their trust toward the harmony of the world which has been previously disrupted by their own unwillingness to witness it and confer a meaning to it. After significant practice, clients develop the ability to recognize their emotions without identifying themselves with any of them (Nhat Hanh, 1992; Hayes et al., 1999). Emotions might still be there with the same intensity, but the client has gained deeper cognition (Damasio, 1995; Davidson et al., 2000; LeDoux, 1996) and awareness about them (Roemer & Orsillo, 2003). The absence of moral judgment in the transition from passive to active intentionality reinforces the clarity of the contact that the client can establish with themselves. If strong fears arise on a passive level, the volitional body would accept and stay with them without judging them as irrational or labeling them as shameful. Conversely, if the client uses small lies or self-deceiving paraphrases to avoid the emotional quality of a certain lived experience, then it would be very difficult for them to recover their self-esteem and an objective outlook on themselves.

Similarly to existential therapy, this intentional acceptance approach tackles the fear of isolation, freedom, and meaninglessness (Watson et al., 1988). A sense of well-being is recovered through the acceptance of the anxiety that is accompanied by this awareness. Yalom 1980, for example, emphasizes the relevance of generating meaning even when these uncertainties become stronger and encourages the immediateness of affective experience in clients. Gendlin (1996) also proposed an approach that was oriented to awareness through acceptance. He argued that the felt sense of bodily sensations can provide individuals with an implied set of reactions to the event itself.

## 2.2 Environments of Anxiety

In the following sections I will describe the interpersonal level of emotional geography. While the previous sections expounded on how personal anxiety can shape the environment, here I will describe two kinds of environment that can raise one's sense of anxiety: one intersubjective and the other virtual.

### 2.2.1 The Intersubjective Environment

Any environment can induce anxiety even when it is explicitly designed to be emotionally neutral or positive. For this reason, to increase the quality of empathy and care we want to have toward others it is important to see the environment through, so to speak, intersubjective eyes. The space of a classroom, for example, can be an example for showing how the anxiety of multiple individuals can resonate with each other and prevent them from achieving the goal for which the class has been conceived. Learning a second language or discussing a moral subject, such as bioethics, can be a challenging task if two or more individuals are plagued by anxiety. In the case of language anxiety, for example, Koch and Terrell (1991, 50) and Young (1992) suggested that classes should become physically smaller in order to let students feel safe in a protective judgment-free environment that would increase the chances of effective exchange and positive interactions. Empirical research (Horwitz et al., 2001) confirmed that many of the reasons for language anxiety are connected to personal and interpersonal beliefs about language learning and an instructor's beliefs about language teaching. Their intersubjective environment is intimately constituted by these beliefs and their normative expectations.

Naturally, time becomes an important quality of the physical space, too. The pace of the classroom's life and its lessons tend to have a strong impact on the level of anxiety of the students. For example, Olympia della Flora, a principal in a disadvantaged school in Columbus, Ohio, understood how important it was for the students to work in smaller classes and to have a calming area duly equipped where they could transition from the stressful familiar environment of home to the learning environment at school. In this school, 98% of the students were in poverty, many of them were homeless or without stable housing; this means that just the simple act of arriving at school was a struggle.[6] They could not feel safe in any environment. Olympia della Flora learned from her students to see the physical structure of the school through their emotional eyes and to redesign the school's classrooms accordingly. The school had to become a safe space where everyone could feel free to express their own anxiety and anger without putting themselves and others in danger. For example, to let the students be free to express their anxiety without having the teachers urging them to stop and repress the feeling, they placed on each desk stress-relieving fidgets that looked like toys; the students were free to hold the toy in their hands and fidget with it. Moreover, they placed little noiseless elliptical machines underneath their desks that allowed students to move their legs during lessons without disturbing anyone. Besides the very useful introduction of meditation classes and/or yoga lessons, I believe that these structural interventions on the environment's inter-subjective space in our daily lives are essential to increasing the quality of our care toward each other. We need to understand how the environment is actually seen and felt by the persons who inhabit it in order to make space for real improvements. Since each environment is constituted by the feelings, sensations, thoughts, and values of an intersubjective group of participants, it is important for each individual to keep open the channel for co-participation. The environment must change with the time and the emotional/geographical issues that are in-volved within the different areas; social anxiety and rage are just some of the many emotional issues that can be addressed at school and in other intersubjective environments in order to increase the quality of our daily lives.

### 2.2.2 How Does a Virtual Environment Affect Anxiety?

Our geography is expanding and we have not yet set in place a clear range of rules to regulate our coexistence in the new space. The system of email storage, social media, voice email, search engines, and clouds in which we exist has become a sort of a transcendental space of our existence. By transcendental I mean the condition of possibility for us to be who we are. At work, a client will look at our profile before making an appointment or, in private life, it is our profile on online dating applications that tell others who we are. Our concrete possibility to express who we are, professionally and personally, often relies on the virtual space. These virtual spaces have often become the space that makes it possible to be what we are; a transcendental space. This invisible environment is growing in importance around us but its virtuality and intangibility does not make its flaws less concerning.

### 2.2.2.1 Digital Health

How does the transcendental quality of this environment affect the existential anxiety we nurture toward our being? As anything pertaining to virtuality, environments, too, have positive and negative effects and it is the job of the bioethicists to lessen the negative ones. Digital mental health, for example, seems to have positive effects in that it reduces anxiety because of the access to services (Musiat et al., 2014); the rapid growth of machine learning technology provides the client with an education about the problem and basic information for self-help (Cowpertwait & Clarke, 2013; Richards & Richardson, 2012); the ability to connect with other people all over the world allows a democratic use of information and a higher quality of health care. An example of this is Dr. Lisa Sanders' New York Times column that puts people of different cultures, countries, and educational backgrounds in contact with each other in order to increase the diagnostic capacity for solving a certain problem. Digital health, in this case, gives access to the best health care possible even to people who live in remote rural areas who otherwise would not have any access (Demaerschalk et al., 2009). There is no longer need for the physical building to host care.

Chris Dancy (2018) summarized three main reasons for which technology in social media can help to lower one's level of emotional anxiety. One, if you are in the middle of a panic attack, you can check on the internet and see that the symptoms you are feeling do not relate to any deadly disease but to an anxiety disorder. The Department of Health in the UK, for example, has started a program called "Putting all of us in control of the health and care information we need,"[7] which is precisely suited to the purpose of giving everyone free emotional education so that they may better care for themselves. The same can be said of the Kaiser Permanente programs in California that use their digital delivery platforms to provide educational videos, chat videos, instant messaging, and forums in order to assure a more affordable and accessible care that connects patient and doctor (De Jong et al., 2015). Secondly, watching videos of people experiencing similar attacks of anger can help to increase empathy and reduce the distance with which one perceives the other, thus limiting one's own fears to more reasonable hypotheses. Third, the applications one uses could be taken as a sort of emotional journal that tells us what sustains our lower or higher moods. For example, Dancy (2018) noticed that the days in which he feels sadder he spends more time on Facebook, while those in which he feels better he spends more time on Evernote or applications that help him to be productive. So, if one is not ready to go to a professional the digital environment might help to keep track of one's own mood swings, to mirror them in others' people experiences (Callahan & Inckle, 2012; Apolinario-Hagen & Vehreschild, 2016), and reduce the sense of stigmatization around the problem.

On the other hand, more specialized education is needed to help us learn how to handle the new virtual space. Medical apps need to be accompanied by regulations that clearly state what can be published on the internet and how they can be implemented, if necessary; at school young students should re- ceive training that educates them to recognize the good sources and separate them from the bad ones (Nochomovitz & Sharma, 2017–18). For example, the Internet, if not used well, can magnify the intensity of hypochondriac attacks when wrong sources are consulted. Critics of digital and telemedicine have noticed how virtual clinicians will depersonalize the already heavily reductionist interaction between patient and doctor, thus eroding the possi- bility for any authentic therapeutic relationship (Lupton & Maslen, 2017; Chaet et al., 2017), as well as impacting the chances for an accurate diagnosis (Fleming et al., 2009). If it is true that technology reduces the distances be- tween patience and doctor, it is also true that it erodes the space of the clinical encounter; "the face of the other" conveys important information that risks getting lost in the virtual environment (Levinas, 1984).

## 2.2.2.2 Anxiety and Social Media

Another virtual space that risks eroding the natural space of mutual encounters is social media. In 2018, approximately two-thirds of US adults were Facebook users, and about two-thirds of these users visited the site at least once a day (Smith & Anderson, 2018). Studies show the strong connection between the use of Facebook, Instagram, Tik Tok and the rise of social anxiety (Huang, 2017); cyber- bullying, media-contagion, the development of unhealthy habits within extreme communities (Luxton et al., 2012) can increase the risk of suicide. A recent work cited by Facebook itself (Ginsberg & Burke, 2017) proved how the passive use of social media, for example, reading posts or other people's pages, can decrease the quality of a person's mood and raise the sense of anxiety in contrast to an interactive and engaging use of it (Burke & Kraut, 2016). Some Silicon Valley developers have themselves called for a greater focus on the ethics of technology design, calling for a "Hippocratic Oath for tech" aimed at protecting people's emotional and psy- chological well-being.[8] As Wu (2006), an internet legal scholar, has noticed, social media's most important currency is attention whose continuous manipulation has shown to have impoverishing effects on psychological experiences and inter- personal relationships. For this reason, Facebook, for example, committed to increasing emotionally healthy ways to connect by focusing the use of the space on the relationship you can have with the people rather than the attention you can pay to or receive from others. Hence, notifications will be focused on what other people in your circle of close friends are doing rather than how many people have seen you or liked you in any way.

## 2.2.3 Normalizing the Environment: Sociale Mediome

One last problematic example of the relationship between individuals' emotions and the environment concerns the cosmetic application of science for the purpose of normalizing an emotionally problematic environment. For example, there is a growing use of medical products to normalize reality according to common parameters: Ritalin and Adderall for deficit of attention, Paxil and Nardil for social phobia (medicalized shyness), cosmetic facial surgery for children with down syndrome, and so on. As mentioned above, any form of environment—virtual, intersubjective, natural—can become a normative set of expectations to which we feel we have to adapt to in order to be how we should be.[9] Clearly, if the normative expectation does not meet the actual substance of our character the body/mind split takes place and gives rise to some of the disorders mentioned above. This becomes even more important if we consider the likely creation of a "sociale mediome" (Eichstaedta et al., 2018; Asch et al., 2015; De Choudhury et al., 2013) which, by using data coming from applications and social media, tracks the health trends, diagnoses illnesses, and predicts behavior such as suicide or depression of the entire society sliced into different geographical areas. Similar to how a genome—a collection of an organism's genetic information—can inform potential risk factors for developing a certain health condition or disease, the scientists working on this project believe that an individual's social mediome can elucidate important insights, like behaviors and repeated exposures that over time can have an impact on a person's health status. I believe it is useful to have an understanding of the medical condition of specific geographic areas in order to prepare institutions to face problems and cope with difficulties that might arise; but, on the other hand, these data cannot set expectations of the kind of well-being that need to be met for the individual to be recognized as healthy. If the project would be successful, then chances are that individuals would find other reasons to split from their body and environment (and increase, consequently, their level of anxiety) since an external, and not a bodily source, would tell them what it means to feel good. Moreover, other bioethical concerns, mostly concerning privacy[10] and health insurance, should be taken into consideration with the creation of a sociale mediome. In fact, the data might be used by insurance companies to predict behaviors and negatively impact the coverage of certain individuals. There are more bioethical concerns around the emerging environments in medicine,[11] but in this chapter we chose to focus only on the impact that they might have on anxiety disorders and their geographical environment.

## Conclusion

In this chapter, I examined the emotional geography of anxiety in order to show the way in which the emotional blockage triggered by anxiety has the power to annihilate the environment and transform its reality into a black hole in which the individuals disappear. Through the analysis of a case study I have shown the steps that the individual can take to recover the interconnection between their body and the environment and overcome the anxious state. The steps involve an intentional reconnection of body and mind, as well as an unconditional acceptance from the individual of their psychophysical vulnerability. In the second part of the chapter, I examined the intersubjectivity of the physical and virtual environments. I have explained how schools, for example, can increase the quality of care toward their students by paying attention to their emotional view of the learning space. This approach revealed to be particularly helpful for disadvantaged students who were suffering from anxiety and anger issues. I examined how less tangible intersubjective environments such as the virtual space of a chat room or the virtual medical office of a doctor can be both beneficial and detrimental to our well-being. Hence, a bioethics meant to foster a good quality of life needs to take into consideration these emotional and environmental factors; any form of detachment from the environment increases the chances of a poor quality of life.

## Notes

1 As I wrote in my *Human Emotions and the Origins of Bioethics*, by scientistic I mean this overgrowth trust in an objective science independent of human beings and yet capable of fixing any of their problems.
2 See, Galway et al. (2019), online: "The year 2018 had the largest number of papers published (17%) suggesting a growing interest in solastalgia since the early 2000s. It should be noted that our review only covered articles published between January and October 2018, and therefore did not capture the full year. The use of the concept is not confined to a specific discipline; the solastalgia literature spans a wide range of academic disciplines, including public health, human geography, anthropology, and philosophy."
3 See, IPCC press release: "In October 2018, the Intergovernmental Panel on Climate Change issued a special report on the impacts of global warming of 1.5 °C [14]. Soon after, the Fourth National Climate Assessment was issued by 13 U.S. federal agencies and presented a stark warning for climate change consequences [15]. In December 2018, the 24th Conference of the Parties to the United Nations Framework Convention on Climate Change (COP24) outcomes highlighted the importance of staying within the 1.5 °C temperature rise target, as well as planning for how to achieve this goal" retrieved from https://www.ipcc.ch/site/assets/uploads/2018/11/pr_181008_P48_spm_en.pdf.
4 See, Orsilio, Roemer, 2015, 15: "Anxiety disorders are in fact the most commonly experienced class of mental health problems in the United States (Narrow et al., 2002), with a conservative estimate of the 1-year prevalence for any disorder of 13.1% for adults aged 18–54. Moreover, many anxiety disorders are associated with a chronic course (e.g., Hirschfeld, 1996; Kessler et al., 1995) and diminished quality of life as evidenced by higher rates of financial dependence, unemployment (e.g., Leon et al., 1995), poorer

quality of life (Massion et al., 1993), and increased risk for completed suicide (Allgulander, 1994). The annual cost of anxiety disorders in the United States in 1990 was estimated to be approximately $42.3 billion or $1,542 per individual with the vast majority of the cost deriving from nonpsychiatric (54%), psychiatric (31%), and pharmacological (2%) treatment (Greenberg et al., 1999). The average health care costs for individuals with anxiety disorders are double those of patients without those disorders even after adjusting for medical comorbidity (Simon et al., 1995)."

5 See, Orsilio, Roemer, 2015, 38: "Although slower to emerge in the clinical psychological literature, the importance of emotion has been embraced within numerous fields of psychology, including development (e.g., Eisenberg et al., 2000), cognition (e.g., Gray, in press), social interaction (e.g., Lopes et al., 2004), abilities and expertise (e.g., Mayer et al., 1999), and neurobiological function (e.g., LeDoux, 1995)."

6 From the transcript: "We went out into the neighborhoods. We had staff meetings in some of the local businesses or the churches. And we would walk to that location as a staff. And then we would say, like, how did you feel about walking through this neighborhood, you know? And they're like, oh, I was really scared. Or, you know, there's really tall grass—they don't even cut the grass. I said, so imagine if you are a 5 or a 6-year-old that has to walk to school through this every single day. How are they feeling by the time that they get to us?" Relieved from https://www.npr.org/transcripts/760255759.

7 Department of Health (2012). The power of information. Putting all of us in control of the health and care information we need. Retrieved from http://webarchive.nationalarchives.gov.uk/20130802094648/https://www.gov [Accessed on: 25/11/16].

8 See the Center for Humane Technology, http://humanetech.com.; Bosker, "The Binge Breaker."

9 See on this point, for example, Frasier's critique of capitalism (2018).

10 It remains unclear the extent to which these data can be used to track human behaviors. See P. A. Clark, K. Capuzzi, and J. Harrison, "Telemedicine: Medical, Legal and Ethical Perspectives," *Medical Science Monitor* 16, no. 12(2010): 261–72; D. W. Bates, A. Landman, and D. M. Levine, "Health Apps and Health Policy: What Is Needed?," *Journal of the American Medical Association* 320, no. 19 (2018): 1976.

11 Although we are focusing in this chapter on the relation between anxiety and social media, the concerns can go beyond this point. See, for example, Terrasse, M., Gorin, M., Sissin, D., 2019, online: "the impact of social networking sites on the doctor-patient relationship, the development of e-health platforms to deliver care, the use of online data and algorithms to inform health research, and the broader public health consequences of widespread social media use. In doing so, we review previous discussions of these topics and emphasize the need for bioethics to focus more deeply on the ways online technology platforms are designed and implemented. We argue that bioethicists should turn their attention to the ways in which consumer engagement, bias, and profit maximization shape online content and, consequently, human behavior and health."

# 3

# EMOTIONAL NUMBNESS

## The Paradox of Exclusion

## Introduction

This chapter focuses on the problem of emotional numbness and, in particular, on the paradox of exclusion in which the problem of emotional numbness seems to be caught. Being excluded or feeling excluded from one's own environment triggers a process of self-exclusion for which the individual detaches from their own intimate life in order to humor the external expectations. While in the previous chapters I examined cases in which the individual is detached from their passive life and environment, as in the cases of anxiety and narcissistic patterns, in this chapter I will investigate the active efforts of individuals to integrate into an environment and life that is felt more as an expectation rather than a reality. The chapter will show how sometimes it can be difficult to just be ourselves and how dangerous it can be to exclude one's own self from one's intimate life. It seems, in fact, that such a choice can lead to a form of numbness that has the power to distort our sense of reality to the point that even the reality of our own body would disappear.

Although emotional numbness can be an important component of a depressive state, this chapter will focus only on emotional numbness. Hopefully, aiming a magnifying glass at this particular component of the problem of depression might eventually bring answers for the larger picture, as well.

## 3.1 Emotional Numbness in Personal Life

Getting out of bed, taking a shower, having breakfast, interacting with people, going to work, this is a daily routine that normally we go through effortlessly without paying too much attention to it, yet these trivial tasks can look like an interminable list of duties for a person who suffers from emotional numbness. Since emotional numbness is a component of different emotional problems but it is not itself considered a disorder, the literature around it is quite limited.[1] Treatments address mostly the major disorders to which emotional numbness is adjacent, that is depression and anxiety.[2] Yet, spontaneous groups have been formed online to talk specifically about emotional numbness and to address its characteristics in order to find a way to cope with it and feel less lonely. For this reason, I will start my analysis by using these online testimonials to provide a description as faithful as possible to the components of emotional numbness.

### 3.1.1 The Beige Feeling

In the following online interaction, we can find different descriptions of the problem of numbness[3]; one of my favorites depicts numbness as "the beige feeling."

"I was severely traumatized as a 12 year old and shut down emotionally. I turned to self harm just so i could feel something other than the overwhelming numbness that had taken over me. Over the ensuing years i was able to experience brief moments of joy - when i held my baby - but these occasions were rare. But i could physically feel depressed, despair, hopelessness even though i was still numb. Now 40 years down the track I want to start feeling joy, love, enjoyment but dont know how to. The numbness is so much a part of how i am that i dont know how to be any different."

"Omg thanks for sharing! ðŸ'• That explains my feelings or lack of. It's horrible when I can't enjoy in the moment my kids my life.. just feel numb xx"

This short exchange is very interesting for several reasons. In the first text, both the style and its content seem to point to a limit of vital engagement that the woman feels in relation to what she is doing. Despite her English seeming to be quite good, she leaves the personal pronoun 'I' in small letters and does not use apostrophes for 'dont'. Similarly, she writes that she cannot engage fully with the experiences that were supposed to make her feel happy, such as holding her child. Several years after her traumatic experience she wants to regain contact with her good emotions again, but for her to do so she needs to bid farewell to a portion of herself as the numbness became too big a part of who she was. She felt overwhelmed by herself.

Sartre's notion of Nothingness, here, can come in handy to describe the reality of what is overwhelming for this woman (2010). For Sartre, Nothingness is not just a concept or a personal fantasy in which someone prefers hiding in order to avoid dealing with daily commitments (Catalano, 2010). From the point of view of Nothingness being an existence is a pretense:

"[W]hat *are we* then if we have the constant obligation to make ourselves what *we are* if our mode of being is having the obligation to be what we are?" (Sartre, 2010, 100)

This woman felt the obligation of being happy when she held her child; this obligation only increased the distance between herself and her own existence. Her existence had become a "representation for herself and for others" (Sartre, 2010, 102–3). "But if I represent myself as him I am not he. I am separated from him as the object from the subject, separated by *nothing* but this nothing isolates me" (Sartre, 2010, 102–3). This separation that excludes the individual from its own self, this Nothingness, is the overwhelming numbness that this person described. The response that so strongly resonated with the other woman confirmed the pretense by which both feel obligated to comply: "I have to be happy with my baby." In this sense, feelings become regulative meanings, haunting expectations rather than the spontaneous outcome of a meaningful interaction. For this reason, everything is perceived as a duty; even a warm shower that many might experience as a treat becomes a haunting duty to accomplish on a daily basis. Every small action creates a horizon of internal expectations that the subject feels obliged to absolve otherwise its own being would disappear.

"It takes a lot of courage and willpower to get out of bed on a tough day, you inspire me! It's so hard to explain this struggle to those who haven't experienced it."

The person who feels emotionally numb is in a constant struggle to be present to their own self even in the simplest, and potentially most joyful moments, of their life. Yet, every action he or she takes risks amplifying the distance already present in relation to their own being because of the pretense that it takes for this common task to be performed.

"Wow, I feel numb … I make attempts to go to work (need money, to pay bills, etc.) First day at work, ok .. this is ok … 2nd day at work-I don't want to go *add excuse* the feeling is strong, my one foot in front of the other, won't budge … I don't want to go … My reasoning-have to pay bills, etc … I have to go … But I DON'T WANT TO GO …

I talk to my daughter, she says, I need to take my lexapro, daily.. I did skip out … so .. I am hoping this antidepressant is going to help me… stop doing this, destructive thing."

As we can see in this passage, the person was aware of their own numbness but could not do anything substantial about it. Emotional numbness is often associated with depression in that emotional numbness can be one of the causes that blocks the vital energy of an individual thus causing a state of depressive moods. Emotional numbness stops the flow of regulative emotions; it can be seen as a silent demand for a real connection between the person and its intimate self. Yet, the Nothingness, that is, the pretense to be who we are not in that moment, creates a distance that is reinforced by the way in which society is structured: we do need to go to work, pay bills, and be social. To use another example, a client of mine was so used to performing and living her life according to the expectation of her family that in order to protect her real self she used to imagine the life she wanted before going to sleep for at least one hour. She would put together a full story with consistency and continuity. Each time she went to sleep or woke up she would pick up where she left off. She came to my office because she was clearly experiencing important intimate issues with her husband and a sense of numbness in her affective life.

So, the main problem is how do we create and defend a legitimate space for ourselves in which we can feel how we really feel? Can we be numb even if we conduct a regular life?

"I MAKE myself get out of bed every day because numbness can set in silently and quicker than I realize sometimes."

"Sometimes is a relief. Crying unexpectedly is awful, but when you become numb .... that is scary".

This person clearly showed how she tried to keep up with a normal life and stick to her daily duties in order to fight off any possible onset of numbness because becoming numb was scarier than feeling depressed. People suffering from clinical depression or chronic disease find sadness a momentary relief from numbness. Feeling numb, in fact, is scarier than any other bad feeling and it spreads out through the body quite fast. Often numbness extends to physical sensations as we will discuss in more detail in the next section. Yet, fighting off numbness through daily discipline can increase the chances of feeling numb because no relevant contact is established with the true parts of ourselves.

"My numbness spread into being physically numb. No pain - none. It was scary weird. I knew I should have my normal aches and pains, I had none. I somewhat " more well " now. I am thankful for the physical pain - sometimes-lol .... depression- it can literally do and effect anything it wants. What a terrible thing it is".

As I will discuss in more detail in the next section, the mind/body whole is such that not only the mind but also the body disappears into the Nothingness. "The body cannot be there for me transcendent and known" (Sartre, 2010, 434) because of the distance that separated my agent self from my real self. Even the physical substance of my body cannot reach my self anymore because my agency is not willing to accept who I really am and acknowledge my existence as it is. As I will explain later in the chapter, one of the most effective ways to cope with this Nothingness would be through acceptance of the bodily and emotional qualities that it expresses:

"Numbness comes for me near my bottom. So I realize I'm numb, then to try to fight back to feeling good, I have to go thru all the feelings-so it's numb, then sad-all the time, then maybe mad or whatever other negative feelings, and in time, there are glimpses of happy and positive feelings. It's a fight to keep moving in that direction. Hoping once I get there, I can learn how to fight to stay there, rather than back and forth so much".

Being able to accept this beige feeling without charging it with any regulative meaning is the best path for reducing the distance. Moreover, people who suffer from numbness tend to predict the extent of their future emotional state in a more objective and accurate way than people in other emotional conditions (Gilbert et al., 1998; Wilson et al., 2004) thanks to their relatively unemotional affective forecasts (Gilbert et al., 2002; Van Boven & Loewenstein, 2003).

"I become apathetic towards everyone and everything. I know it will eventually end but it takes all of my resources (faith, family, psychologist, psychiatrist and medications as well as a rare hospitalization) to pull me through the numbness and despair. It's a terrible, invisible disease but it CAN be overcome".

The ability to see the affective boundaries of this mental state allows the individual to release the shame that is often attached to any emotional disorder. The shame of being too much for others (Lo, 2018) is one of the most common reasons for which people prefer embracing loneliness instead of trying to establish a real connection around them in real life. As explained in my *Human Emotions and the Origins of Bioethics,* chapters 2 and 3, emotions are a nourishing part of our living system; if we lose these nutrients, our vitality and accordingly our chance to take part in a real life would decrease. If the connection with our body is missing, our desire to live would significantly decrease as the following passage shows:

"That's interesting that you feel that too. I had to explain to someone that when I feel nothing I don't eat. I'm looking for a way to feel anything."

The physical valence of emotional numbness is so strong that it significantly impacts our organic life and our vitality. We lose appetite. We cannot sleep. We cannot move. The emotionally numb individual might feel indifferent toward all the sensuous and material things that were attractive before because the relevant connections with their organic body are lost in the growing distance between their agent self and their own body.

"I also find it almost impossible to eat when I've been like this, too. Nothing is appealing - not even my favorite foods. And anything too heavy/rich/flavorful makes me feel (no matter how little) slightly revolted, even. It's awful".

### 3.1.2 The Paradox of Exclusion

At the basis of the emotional numbness lies an excruciating paradox: the person who was excluded from an intimate nurturing life (mostly because of a traumatic event) is the same one who excludes themselves from their own intimate space. Even if feeling something is often considered better than the nothingness-feeling, it is quite difficult, if not impossible, for many of these people to allow themselves to feel that connection.

When a person experiences emotional numbness the Diagnostic and Statistical Manual of Mental Disorders, 5th Edition (DSM V) tells us that this person might also suffer from panic attacks, depression, drug intoxication, persistent complex bereavement disorder, PTSD, acute stress disorder, dissociative identity disorder, or depersonalization/derealization. What does that mean? It is very likely that at the origin of numbness there is a very old traumatic experience that has led the individual to exclude him/herself from their own intimate life and create an alternate paler reality (Spiegel et al., 2017) where to live. Except for those who experience numbness because of drug abuse and medications (Read et al., 2014), emotional numbness might result from a disruptive coping mechanism (Sandell & Bornäs, 2015) against strong emotions (Kennedy & Ceballo, 2016). In order to defend herself from painful feelings the individual has closed the door to her feelings (Sedeño et al., 2014). Any intimate connection with her inner self is impossible; as a consequence, the fertile soil of life does not have the chance to nourish with energy the individual. Hence, the vitality that emotionally numb people experience is quite low. Yet, despite there being an underground sense of desperation from which they would like to escape, they do not feel like they have enough energy to open the door to that trauma and to acknowledge their feelings again.

The trauma excluded themselves from the affective circle of their family, society, friends, and personal intimacy. Now they exclude themselves from their own intimate life and, accordingly, from a beneficial connection with their emotional and geographical environment. A witness remains but in the form of a stranger that looks at that life from an external point of view.

### 3.1.3 Carl and His Ethical Riddles

When Carl contacted me, it was because he needed help with ethical reasoning. Carl was a successful professional of 45 with a scientific, practical mind and a troubled marriage. He felt emotionally numb to everything and everyone and did not understand the reasoning behind his own actions. His marital crisis began when he had inappropriate interactions with other women without his wife knowing. He did not enjoy these interactions, instead finding everything quite sad. He considered his wife much more beautiful than the other women and claimed to still be in love with her. He could not understand why he decided to push himself to do the things that he did. He shared his experiences with his wife who felt very hurt by his behavior. At that point he decided to contact me because he did not want to lose her.

After our short introductory phone conversation, my instincts told me that it was better to start with individual encounters rather than jumping into couples sessions. His real concern seemed to be more focused on the ethical motives behind his actions rather than on the dynamics between the two of them. He was a sort of a puzzled witness of his own life. We met consistently for two months. He was very eager to discover the reasons for his emotional blockage and sounded ready to work on himself. The first core problem that emerged in his relationship with his wife was trust. He told me that he could trust only his brother and no one else.

Although Carl and his wife had been together for 15 years, he could not trust her fully; without that trust, his wife felt that they could not work together as a team.

This was a very vicious circle for a married couple. Following the path of trust was particularly revealing for our work together. Carl could trust his brother because only his brother had witnessed the same traumatic experiences as Carl, those of having to endure an abusive father. Growing up, Carl learned that he had to "suck up his emotions and pretend that everything is fine." This meant that from a very young age Carl's life was mainly a pretense. He behaved according to the script that his father and then later his wife demanded from him. He was very distant from himself and, accordingly, from his wife. He also did not have important friends because, like with his wife, he could not trust them.

Carl openly admitted that when he had his romantic trysts with the other women his sense of reality was strongly blurred by fantasy. So much so that the actual encounters were a wake-up call for him. It was this realization that led him to look for emotional help—although he presented the problem mainly as an ethical one.

The way I saw it, the real Carl was acting out in order to regenerate an intimate space with himself, to shock himself into a reaction. At the time we met, he had not yet faced the traumatic experiences of his childhood. I helped him to feel sorry and compassionate for himself when thinking of what he had been through and to detach his inner voice from that of his father. In fact, during our meetings we noticed that his inner moral voice was very similar to that of his abusive father and, occasionally, he projected this same voice onto his wife—leaving her with a sense of frustration because she felt invisible to him. From there we proceeded to remove, as much as possible, the projections of his father on his wife so that he could look at her as a human being and not as the new holder of the script for his life. It was very difficult for him to see the vulnerabilities of his wife at first. Intense sadness emerged after our first encounters but was accompanied by a renewed vital energy that allowed him to plan vacations with his wife and reassure her about the feelings of insecurity that arose in relation to her own body and sexual vigor. The fact that Carl could acknowledge his trauma and release himself from the pretense that he felt obliged to follow allowed him to recognize that his coping mechanisms had to change. The harsh voice that was commenting on all the actions he took covered his real voice and made it difficult to connect with the intersubjective reality of his present life. Although we did not work explicitly on the trust issues, the emotional numbness seemed to have lifted and made space for an enjoyable life with his partner. The non-formalized reality that was suppressed under the weight of the pretense managed to come to the surface and find its own expression. At that point, the ethical motives of Carl's actions no longer seemed so detached from his reality and it was finally possible for him to understand the reasons behind his choices.

## 3.2 What Reality?

In what kind of reality is living the person suffering from emotional numbness? In a beautiful article written in defense of Husserl's realism (1970), Fink addressed the complexity of Husserl's notion of reality. In this article, Fink described the continuity of Husserl's phenomenological project (1970, 74) based on the way in which the philosopher penetrated the concreteness of reality and unfolded its meanings. As Fink stated, genuine phenomenological inquiry begins with "the awakening of an immeasurable wonder over the mysteriousness of the state of affairs [Sachlage] confronting philosophy at its beginning" (Fink, 1970, 109). This concreteness, in fact, refers to the portion of reality that is not formalized yet in any logical meaning but still needs to be clarified. The reality of the world in which we normally live goes unquestioned so does the reality of the person who suffers from emotional numbness, especially if they are playing according to a self-excluding external script. Their intimate reality has lost its concreteness as it became a normative script. According to Fink, both in Husserl's *Ideas* (1913) and *Logical Investigations* (1900), phenomenology's goal is to clarify "everything which can be brought to the point of manifesting itself as it is, be it real or ideal" (1970, 85). In phenomenology, reality refers to two different but related meanings: the intentional reality (in German, *real*—translated in this passage with ideal) of what is believed as true and valuable by the experiencing subject, and the core reality (in German, *reel*) which is conceived of as existing independently of our experiencing of it. On the one hand, stands the real world (*reel*) as it is and, on the other, the world as it is experienced by us (*real*)—these two forms of reality are of course very different from yet interrelated with each other.

When a traumatic experience occurs, these two realities split from each other and generate a distance that impacts the way in which the living person experiences their intimate life and their own environment (*real*). When this core reality is disrupted by traumatic events, the person tends to shut down the access to it and excludes itself from the flow of their own life. At this point, the real world (reel) no longer offers a ground for actual experience; the core space of reality (real) is then replaced by a voice interiorized from the traumatic experience which mostly coincides with self-shame and self-blame. In the case of Carl, he internalized his father's harsh voice and projected it onto his wife. The reality of his core-world (real) should have been nourished by the experience he had of the real world (reel); if this latter failed, as it did with Carl's father, to produce meanings and values that are consistent with his experience of the real world, the daily life becomes an endless and meaningless repetition of the script behind the same traumatic experience. As a sort of echo, the traumatic experience will color all future experiences and will reproduce the same grade of shame, fear, anxiety, and meaninglessness that the ultimate traumatic experience evoked. While this defense mechanism serves the individual to keep the traumatic event frozen at a distance with a low emotional charge, it prevents them from being emotionally nourished by life; the traumatic experience needs to be integrated in the life of the person for that door to the real world to be opened and that experience to be transformed into meanings.

"The world which we know and within which we know ourselves is given as a universe of acceptances", Fink wrote (1970, 107). If there is no acceptance of the traumatic experience the givenness of that world remains suspended. As Fink wrote, "phenomenology does not disconnect the world in order to withdraw from it and occupy itself with some other philosophical thematic, but (…) in order ultimately to know the world" (1970, 115) in its full concreteness and pre-predicative meanings. For this reason, a phenomenological approach could be a good technique for recovering contact with that reality by practicing epoché and reduction (more on this in my *Human Emotions and the Origins of Bioethics*, chapter 3 and in the next section). The individual who is left alone in the core reality (*reel*) needs to be reached out to and lead back to the bridge that keeps *real* and *reel* in communication with each other. That core reality is defined by phenomenology as the transcendental dimension.

## 3.2.1 Psychological Reduction

The transcendental dimension represents that very thin layer of our reality (real) that allows the core reality of the world (reel) as it appears to us to unfold in front of us according to its main characters. The access to the transcendental dimension is grounded in the life-world and in the psychological subject who decides to undertake this kind of search. Exploring this dimension allows us to understand what are the psychological patterns that characterize our own reality and what part of these characters can be transformed into a less excluding and numbing environment. For this reason, phenomenology opens the doors to this space of reflection through reduction. As Fink wrote:

> The phenomenological reduction is not primarily a method of simply disconnecting, but one for leading back. It leads, through the most extreme radicalism of self-reflection, the philosophizing back through itself to the transcendental life of belief whose acceptance-correlate, the world is. In other words, it is the method for discovering and exposing a knowledge-thematic which is in principle nonworldly: the dimension of the origin of the world (1970, 126).

Phenomenological reduction is a form of meditative practice that leads (*ducere*) the reflecting individual back (*re*) to the nonworldly space of pain in which the experiences occurred and generated the intense emotions that are still floating in the air. In this sense, phenomenological and psychological reductions cooperate in clarifying the content of that core reality and question the lack of acceptance of the traumatic experience into the present life. While phenomenological reduction sheds light on the absolute interconnection of the real (reel) and the intentional (real) world, the psychological one illuminates only a region of the interconnectedness, i.e., the psychical one (Husserl, 1923, 118). In the case of emotional numbness, the meanings, affects, and values that emerge after the application of reduction can be recomposed by illuminating the point of inter-connection between the two realities.

The psychological reduction discloses a region of consciousness that is conducive to the phenomenological exploration: "the sphere of my own immanence, as well as the spheres of immanence belonging to other psyches which come to be identified through empathy"[4] (Fink, 1970, 118). For this reason, as mentioned in the previous section, compassionate acceptance of one's own feelings can help to move beyond the sense of numbness. Being empathetic toward oneself is the first step to allowing the interconnection of the two realities to be seen and explored. The psychological reduction delimits "an area within the world, <as> a method for going beyond the world by removing limits" (Fink, 1970, 119). In doing so, the core reality "does not dissolve the world into mere being-for-us in the sense of psychical subjectivity but maintains the existence of things as independent of human knowledge" (Fink, 1988, 187).[5] The psychological subject that applies the reduction wit-nesses both realities, the traumatic one that still impacts the present life and the reality as it unfolds during the lifetime of the individual. In this way, the individual recovers awareness of how their own past reality (real) conditions (in a transcendental way) the constitution of the present reality (reel) according to self-excluding patterns (especially, in the case of people suffering from emotional numbness).

### 3.2.2 A Triadic Ego

The reduction sheds light on a triadic ego. In fact, when applying the epoché, a triadic structure of the ego (psychological, reflexive/practical, and transcendental) emerges. A person's identity remains always the same, that is their feeling emotionally numb is always the same, even though their ego can occupy different positions in time and space. The present ego looks at its past and enters into the eternal space of the emotions that still impact its present and past since emotions are not in a linear time and space. As I noted above, the psychological ego is "the human being who is preoccupied with the world" (Fink, 1970, 115). When the reflexive ego, practicing the epoché, suspends the psychological ego's natural belief in the world, it invites the transcendental ego to reflect on the previous acceptances of the world—in the case of emotional numbness, not all the ac-ceptances occurred because the traumatic event blocked some of them. The reduction itself is part of the egoic structure as a reflexive position that elicits the awakening of the psychological ego. That ego, in fact, needs to awaken in front of the reality of the traumatic experience in order to accept it and transform it into meanings and values. As Fink wrote, the reduction is "a structural moment of the transcendental reflection", "a reflexive moment of refraining from belief on the part of the reflecting observer" (Fink, 1970, 115).

The triadic ego does not imply an actual change within the life of the subject, but an actual repositioning in relation to the meanings that it can grasp and clarify; the state of affairs, philosophically speaking, has not changed. To apply this notion on the case presented above, when Carl looked at his life, he was still Carl witnessing his life from when he was a teenager. The way in which he reflexively reacted as a teenager needed to be overcome by reflection. For this to happen his psychological ego needed to accept (transcendental dimension) what happened and feel for what that teenager had to go through. This repositioning of the ego triggers an ethical and cognitive shift that helps the individual to reconnect with the vitality that has been lost in the disconnection from the real. The ethical shift would be possible exactly because the individual willingly suspends any temptation for self-blaming and self-judgments. "The psychical intention of the psychological ego is essentially receptive; in terms of its own self-illumination, it is performed as a means of gaining access to being which is in itself independent of its intention" (Fink, 1970, 134). The intentionality of the reflecting ego, which Fink called transcendental-act intentionality, indicates the intentionality through which the ego awakens from the ongoing flow of its natural life and reflexively performs the reduction. Finally, the transcendental-constitutive intention is the intentionality of the transcendental ego that generates new patterns to explain the present reality. Any description of these two standpoints is doomed to appear paradoxical to us because it speaks from a layer of time and space that is timeless in itself and hence not aligned with our normative embodied self-experience as psychological subjects (since, when functional, our neurological structure is such to transform each datum into a semantic continuum).[6] Yet we need to cope with that paradox because time is paradoxical in itself and emotions participate in it since they are not attached to the linear sense of time. The pain that Carl felt when he was young was still present in his adult life. Although he has aged, the young Carl kept being there and was still feeling that rage because his feelings had never found a channel to come to meaningful expression.

### 3.2.3 The Time of Emotions

The first two forms of intentionality, the natural life and reflexive awakening, involve a sense of time-space that is difficult to conceive for human beings. The former is an ego-intention situated in a linear sense of time; the latter, transcendental one is situated in an absolute space-time fully disconnected from our beliefs as psychological egos. The absolute time, as its etymology suggests is absolute (from Latin, *ab-solutus*, that is disconnected from) precisely because it is disconnected from our existence as psychological entities.

The transcendental layer of the ego is not actual because it does not locate itself within a mundane time-space but is an absolute whose primordiality can be shortly perceived only through awakenings. Since the transcendental layer is motionless, the awakenings originate from within another egoic layer: the practical or reflexive ego. The directedness of this egoic layer is always alternating between the psychological and the transcendental directions because its nows knit together the two different dimensions of time: linear time and absolute time. The nature of time is such that the phenomenologist who desires to communicate has only worldly concepts at his disposal; that is, the concept of the psychological ego made available through the awakening of the practical ego. In my work with Carl, I asked him to shatter the linearity of his time and look at the absolute time of his emotions which became the vehicle for his awakening to happen. His disposition was fully available to allow the rupture in the linear time; his desperation made him ready to face the intensity of his emotions in the transcendental positioning of his ego. I helped him to translate the concreteness of his timeless emotions into adequate meanings; to do that I set aside any expectations about what was going to happen (epoche), although important limits can be encountered in this exercise. "The mundane meaning of the worlds available to her <the phenomenologist> cannot be entirely removed, for their meaning can be limited only by the use of other mundane words (…). The inadequacy of all phenomenological reports caused by the use of nonworldly meaning also cannot be eliminated by the invention of a technical language (…). Phenomenological statements contain an internal conflict between a word's mundane meaning and the transcendental meaning which serves to indicate" (Fink, 1970, 144). Application of the phenomenological reduction has to take into account this stratification of time and the tensions it yields.

Given the deep interconnectedness of the three layers of time and being, all these three layers can be actively operating in the phenomenological and psychological analyses.[7] Each of these three layers—psychological, (in whose concreteness the transcendental ego dwells), reflexive/practical (whose awakenings and reflexivity are lived by the practical ego), and transcendental (whose natural life corresponds to the patterns that characterize the life of the psychological ego)—are characterized by a different form of time and intentionality which can be described as simultaneously passive, practical, and active; each form of intentionality constitutes reality according to different characteristic marks. In this case, the disposition of Carl was fully open to allow the awakening of the practical ego and connect it to the experienced reality of the traumatic event.

Despite the fact that these intentional stations speak different spatiotemporal and psychological languages, they need each other in order to be. The volitional reflective ego (Husserl, 2002, 284) needs a body with an appropriate neurological structure in order to be able to think and the volitional reflexive being needs a transcendental ego in order to be able to receive, understand, and store information that conditions the patterns with which the body sees reality. The awoken psychological ego, which decides what to accept and negate from the perceived reality, is the practical connection between the two. An effective treatment addresses the full triadic structure taking care of the time-space complexity that it involves. In fact, the interconnection of the real takes place at the same point in time; yet the time itself in that same point has a different meaning (linear, eternal, timeless) and structure (succession of befores-afters, standing being, nothingness). The receptive side of the ego awakens through the awakening of this practical reflexive ego, the reflective, transcendental layer begins the process of constituting meanings from the same point of awakening. When a psychological problem arises, it means that one of these stations (each of them including a specific sense of reality, time, and intentionality) is not in line with the others. My suggestion is for the phenomenological practitioner to "manually" readjust this alignment by eliciting the practical intentionality and awakening through a series of transcendental reductions.

## 3.3 The Consequences of Emotional Numbness at Work: Medical Behavior

Expanding the problem of emotional numbness into the intersubjective territory of public care, Schenk and Roscoe (2017) described bioethics as a field in which emotional numbness can generate relevant problems. Taking emotions into due consideration could potentially have a large and beneficial influence on decisions and interpersonal exchanges. Yet, as it happens with the mechanism of numbing intense emotional reactions, emotions in bioethics are often silenced and rarely exposed to intersubjective judgment. The consequence is that the characters studied in a medical case, for example, seem often mute and the decisions made fully irrational.[8] As in the case of TN:

TN was a baby boy born with multiple congenital anomalies, including alobar holoprosencephaly (HPE), a disease that occurs when the brain does not develop nor divide into the right and left lobe.[9] These cerebral anomalies were diagnosed in utero. TN also had a cleft lip/palate, feeding problems, severe gastroesophageal reflux (GER), failure to thrive, and seizure disorder. TN had the abnormal muscle tone and impaired motor abilities present in virtually all individuals with HPE. TN's mother (age 16) and father (age 20) lived separately with their respective parents. TN was conceived during their very brief romantic relationship, which neither desired to continue. TN's mother dropped out of high school when she found out she was pregnant, and her attempts to complete a High School Equivalency Diploma Program (GED) were not consistently productive, no doubt complicated by the birth of a seriously ill baby. TN's father had also dropped out of high school before graduating and was working part-time as a pizza delivery driver. (Schenk and Roscoe, 2017, 23)

The medical staff described TN's parents behaviors as "minimally interactive" and "antagonistic and hostile" (Schenk and Roscoe, 2017, 24); given the young age of the parents, it is possible that their behavior was due to shame ("their apparent lack of interest in working with the health care team in their son's best interests", Schenk and Roscoe, 2017, 25). After two months, TN was recommended by a neonatologist to have a PEG tube[10] inserted to insure he had sufficient nutrition and hydration. The mother refused to follow this procedure. When TN was six months old, though, she was obliged to leave her baby at the hospital because an extension of a three-day calorie count was needed to keep TN alive. The mother visited him regularly but only in the evenings when doctors were not around, while the father was very irregular with his visits. On day eight, TN was transferred to the Pediatric Intensive Care Unit where, for a second time, they strongly recommended the insertion of a PEG, but they had problems in contacting the mother on the phone. When they finally reached her to communicate the deteriorating condition of TN her answer was "I don't want my baby to have any more things done to him," she said, "We just want him back home with us" (Schenk and Roscoe, 2017, 24). TN never came back home. The PEG was inserted but it did not prevent his condition from worsening; he was put on a ventilator, was in need of blood transfusions, and his nutrition did not improve, even after receiving the PEG. During this time, the mother's visits became much more irregular and TN's father's visits stopped completely. The medical staff tried to reach them with phone calls and texts in order to explain to them the reasons why TN's condition was worsening. The parents came to a meeting once and expressed their feelings of being "forced" to consent to the PEG insertion which led to the rapid decline of their baby (Schenk and Roscoe, 2017, 24). After that meeting they refused to attend others; the extended family of the mother participated in other meetings and in one of these the grandmother stated that "she felt the decisions had been taken out of their hands when TN's mother was 'forced' to consent to the PEG tube; she had, after all, declined it in the past" (Schenk and Roscoe, 2017, 25). Moreover, "She also reiterated that the family would have preferred for the baby to be at home, and she said they were never given that option" (Schenk and Roscoe, 2017, 26). One month after that meeting it became clear that TN was near death. The medical staff unsuccessfully tried to reach the family in the afternoon and the next morning, so the doctors decided to stop the ventilator. TN died within the next few minutes. Later that day, the family came to stay beside TN's death bed where they were given support from pastoral care and child life services.

The young parents felt excluded from the life of their own child. They did not feel as though they were part of a team with the medical care staff because their voices consistently went unheard. Both the parents and the medical staff meant well for TN, but one decision prevailed over the other, the medical over the parental. I believe (and I am not alone in this, Schenk and Roscoe, 2017, 30) that parents need to have the option and support to say "no" to burdensome treatments for their children. The narrative of this case gives us no clue about whether or to what extent such counseling was provided (Schenk and Roscoe, 2017, 28). TN's family seems to have accepted TN's impending death sooner than the medical staff ("God would not let our baby suffer and will take him when it is time" Schenk and Roscoe, 2017, 25) and wanted him home to die (Schenk and Roscoe, 2017, 25). Yet, that option was not available from the beginning.

TN's mother seemed irrational and difficult to understand for the team. In fact, the pain and suffering in which TN's family was living were expressed in emotional numbness and detachment from their part. They preferred to reduce the visits to their son and accept the script of the shameful young parents that seem to have been attached to them by the medical environment from the very beginning. The extended family was more responsive than they were, although by the end they were the ones who openly lamented a coercive attitude from the hospital.

Whose decision was it to let the child die? The physicians' or the parents'? Here it seems that the parents' ages played an important factor in the way in which communications and information were handled; they did not seem to be involved in the decisions that were made by the medical staff. They became emotionally numb and let vital decisions fall first to the extended family and then to the medical personnel. It would be absolutely acceptable to believe that the autonomy and authority of the parents should be respected when it is time to make important decisions about their seriously ill children; yet, as it emerged from this and other cases (Schenk and Roscoe, 2017, 23) little evidence shows that informed input regarding resuscitation and treatment is given (Harrison 2008; Keenan et al. 2005; Partridge et al. 2001). It seems that laws and standard procedures have the final word on this sensitive matter. Similar policies can only increase the emotional pain. We do not know about the financial and psychological efforts with which the family had to cope in order to guarantee TN sufficient care. It does not seem that the family received any of this support while the standard procedures were implemented. Unfortunately, neonatal and pediatric intensive care units have become increasingly important profit centers since the 1990s (Harrison 2008; Simpson 1999; Silverman 1993). Hospital systems have become, in the words of pediatrician Lantos, "hooked on neonatology," with clear incentives to expand medical care options to this new population (2001), which fosters an ethics of aggressive care intervention. It seems that in this case, the parents and the extended family were left financially and psychologically alone thus resulting in the emotionally numb parental attitude that the medical staff lamented. A survey of 149 practicing neonatologists in New England showed how more than half of them saw their role as providing information in a neutral manner; far fewer saw their role as helping parents balance the risks and benefits of treatment or the familial or social consequences of their decisions (Bastek et al. 2005). Another study showed that neonatologists who provided information in a neutral manner left parents feeling isolated; parents preferred support and engagement with the medical care team in the decision-making process (Payot et al. 2007). In TN's case, both sides were suffering: the medical staff was frustrated because important decisions needed to be made in a short time and TN's family was nowhere to be found; TN's family was numb to the medical staff's requests because they felt excluded from important decisions, felt forced out of TN's life, and became foreign to their own responsibilities. The results of that coercive exclusion were, again, to exclude themselves from the life of their child. Overcoming the sense of exclusion could have been a good path to take in order to recompose the problem but as I showed in this chapter, the exclusion paradox seems to be the basis of emotionally numb behavior.

### 3.3.1 Emotional Numbness and Social Exclusion

The paradox of emotional numbness is even more visible in social life (Masicampo, 2009, Baumeister & Leary, 1995). Even though one would imagine that the most immediate reaction to social marginalization is rage or aggressive feelings, the most common reaction to social exclusion is, in fact, marked by emotional numbness and a surprising lack of feeling (Masicampo, 2009, Baumeister & Leary, 1995). Human beings, similarly to animals, respond to rejection with physical numbness (MacDonald & Leary 2005) as they are using the same physiological system with which they learn to freeze when confronted by threats of injury (Panksepp, 1998; Eisenberger et al., 2003). Social rejection challenges the chances of survival for both animals and human beings and the distress that emerges from that bodily awareness produces a freezing-attitude response (Buckley et al., 2004; Williams et al., 2000), which can be expressed in a wide range of social behaviors (Baumeister et al., 2002; Buckley et al., 2004). Forcing anyone to foreign expectations is rarely lamented and denounced because the victim would most likely slip into a state of quiet numbness instead of fighting off.

### 3.3.1.1 The Paradox as a Social Mechanism

The paradox of exclusion is triggered by the acceptance of the very first exclusion. If one accepts being excluded, then this person will exclude him/herself from the flood of feelings and emotions that the primal exclusion triggered. The first exclusion triggers a chain of more and more painful exclusions that duplicate the distance between the person and their own reality. Her reality is lost and so is the possibility to access her intimate space. Emotional numbness is the result of this impasse (Baumeister et al., 2005; Gardner et al., 2000; Twenge et al., 2001; Zadro et al., 2004).

According to Masicampo (2009), emotional numbness activates the body's pain system which alters the individual's response to emotions (Eisenberger et al., 2003). For this reason, rejected people experience low sensitivity to physical pain (MacDonald & Leary, 2005) and a number of negative health consequences.[11] A link between social and physical pain exists (Herman & Panksepp, 1978; Panksepp et al., 1978) that activates neural mechanisms whose original purpose is to detect and regulate physical pain. The anterior cingulate cortex (ACC), which is designed to warn the human body about alarming factors or threats present in their environment (Bush et al., 2000; Eisenberger & Lieberman, 2004; Nelson &

Panksepp, 1998), helps in detecting social exclusion (Masicampo, 2009) as it threatens the correct human functioning in its environment.

## 3.3.1.2 The Paradox: Shutting Down the Body

Another example of this paradox is the case of Matt Lee divulged by Lisa Sanders in her New York Times column. Matt presented feelings of deja vu before fainting; during some of these episodes his heart would stop completely. The doctors tested him for temporal lobe epilepsy and vasovagal syncope, but they did not find in any of them the actual reason for his fainting. Through her column, Dr. Sanders opened the diagnostic process to a wide number of people belonging to different fields of expertise. The more convincing diagnosis came from psychology which explained the fainting as related to anxiety disorder. In his interviews, in fact, Matt repeatedly stated how difficult his family was for him. Although that symptom was not taken into serious consideration when making a diagnosis, the anxiety he felt in relation to his family seemed to be the most important epiphenomenon of his problem. Matt, in fact, used to live with his grandma as his father left soon after his birth and his mother was very discontinuous in the care she provided for him. According to the interviews of Matt's parents and his nana, Matt seemed to have been excluded from his parents' care in very early childhood. After he was born, his parents split. His father moved hours away from him and lost contact with Matt until Matt's mother, without a home or a job, asked Matt's father to take care of him. They agreed on a temporary solution. Suddenly, Matt found himself living in a place that was not his own with a person that he did not recognize as his parent. It is interesting to notice how some of the deja vu encounters that he would experience in his adult life, would take him back to those memories right before blacking out. Before fainting, he could not understand, in fact, why the image of certain cartoons would come to his mind. Later on, he realized that those were the cartoons he used to watch at his father's house.

Without receiving full consent from the father, Matt's nana put him on a flight back to her house. Although Matt seemed to be very happy to rejoin the familiar face of his nana, the experience was undoubtedly traumatic. As the recurring bouts of deja vu showed, his childhood strongly impacted the quality of his adult life. Although in the video interview his manners seemed very calm and resigned, that calmness seemed to reflect the emotional numbness that he had built to shield himself from the pain over the years. Behind that calmness, Matt's bodily system was strongly impacted even though he was not able to feel anything. The sense of isolation in which Matt grew up impacted his health. Traumatic events like the one experienced by Matt can be thoroughly heartbreaking, especially if the person is made to feel numb from that experience. People may report feeling "hurt" or "crushed" after the dissolution of a friendship or romantic relationship (Leary & Springer, 2001), that feeling can extend beyond metaphor since social and physical pain operate using the same neural mechanism (MacDonald & Leary, 2005). In this case Matt recovered through cognitive-based psychotherapy. As I am writing this, Matt can still feel the same symptoms approaching as before but he can slow down the anxiety and prevent the actual fainting. Anxiety and other negative emotional states after rejection and ostracism can severely impact one's physical well-being (Baumeister & Tice, 1990; Leary, 1990; Williams et al., 2000).

### 3.3.2 Environmental Numbness

In terms of environmental care, it might happen that people suffering from emotional numbness due to social exclusion or solastalgia (see chapter 2 on this concept) behave in a less prosocial manner compared toward others and the common environment (Twenge et al., 2007); empathy and prosocial behaviors are increased, in fact, if social help is received (Batson et al., 1995). Thus, it is possible that social exclusion might temporarily disable the capacity for strong empathic reactions to the distress of one's self and others (Masicampo, 2009). An environment of emotionally numb people is a non-vital environment if the energy of everyone is blocked behind a shield of self-exclusion. Since the body reacts to social exclusion in the same manner as it does to physical injury (DeWall & Baumeister, 2006), emotionally numbed people might experience reduced empathy for the suffering of others. In general, it is quite probable that persons who struggle with daily tasks and feel disconnected from their own body would struggle to engage with social and environmental issues (Weber, 2017).

This form of disconnection between human beings and their environment is, unfortunately, a common, everlasting problem (e.g., see Rockström et al., 2009; Steffen et al., 2015). The birth of disciplines such as conservative psychology and ecological psychology, came as a way to fill the gap and prevent a disastrous outcome from occurring. Different studies, for example, showed how climate change has had a dramatic impact on the way in which we make decisions, execute plans, and behave (Lorenzoni et al., 2005). Other studies proved how environmental changes affect the way in which we perceive emotions and reciprocate them (Boynton et al., 2019). Yet, according to a study conducted by the Australian Psychological Society, there is still 8% of the population across the US, UK, and Australia that denies the reality of climate change. According to this study "Can science denial be stopped by first explaining the psychological research into why and how people deny climate science" (Cook, 2012; Hamilton, 2010; Hulme, 2009; Lewandowsky et al., 2013) and activating their feelings toward themselves and their needs.

The water crisis is a clear example of this. John Thorson wrote, "Water links us to our neighbor in a way more profound and complex than any other" (cited in Ziervogel, 2019). In January 2018, Cape Town announced it was close to the "Day Zero" of their water capacity. A city of four million people was three months away from one of the biggest possible ecological disasters, "the largest drought-induced municipal water failure in modern history." (cited in Ziervogel, 2019). Ninety days prior to "Day Zero" the disaster was averted by transforming human indifference toward ecological problems into active collaboration. Vierzogel, who worked actively to avert the crisis, condensed the lesson learnt from this water crisis in an interesting paper.[12]

The core of these 12 lessons was to sensitize the city to water supplies and water value. When the city woke up from its state of numbness and shock, people came together and started cooperating with each other. The national government allocated water supplies in the region at risk, imposed taxes on water consumption, farmers agreed to divert additional water stored for agricultural purposes to the city, and Cape Town launched a city-wide water map to show water consumption on a household level, allowing people to compare their consumption to their neighbors and the rest of the city.

> Nine of the lessons identify what needs to be put in place before a crisis hits to strengthen preparedness. Build systems and relationships of mutual accountability for effective water management between spheres of government. Strengthen collaboration across departments within municipalities through strong trust-building leadership, instilling a culture of collaboration enabled through the necessary structures with associated lines of accountability
>
> *(Ziervogel, 2019, passim)*

The Cape Town crisis was averted because people became responsible for their choices, broke their sense of numbness, and initiated a collaboration toward a common intersubjective good.

There are numerous examples of how the fog of emotional numbness prevents our relationships with our closest ones from flourishing and our environment from being fully lived and liveable. Emotional numbness makes us believe that we are not part of any basic relationship and our very being is lonely and detached from any complex living system. Once again, we are excluded and we exclude ourselves. Similarly to people who struggle to feel emotions like appetite, joy, or pain, we struggle to connect with what it really means to run out of water, to have no more air to breathe, or to lose the flora and fauna that make our globe livable. Time, again, plays an important role in this form of social exclusion; the linear sense of time leads us to believe that we will not be there when the crisis hits us, yet the eternal and present sense of time tells us the opposite. Our emotional struggles are proof of the impossible living conditions we impose on ourselves in the present. Every careless or harmful action we take toward or against the environment increases our distance from the environment, which harms us psychologically and physically. This distance, in fact, reinforces that same numbness that undermines our psychological and physical well-being.

## Conclusion

This chapter focused on the paradox of exclusion which characterizes emotional numbness. Traumatic experiences might lead one to feel excluded. This primal exclusion reflects on a deeper form of exclusion according to which the same person who was once excluded excludes, then, themselves from their own intimate space and starts living a life according to an external social script. This chapter showed how this dynamic reflects not only on the level of personal life, creating emotional numbness and eventually depression, but also on a social and biological level: a water crisis or antisocial behaviors in the professional life are some of the examples presented in this chapter. Cases that range from personal life to medical dilemmas were used to show what kind of reality emotional numbness gives shape to and how that impacts the life we conduct in our environment. Breaking emotional numbness through reconnection with one's own intimate life could be conducive to recuperating one's vitality, both in their personal and social lives. The phenomenological use of reduction was proposed as a method to shed light on the complex time and space reality of the hurtful emotions that hide behind the primal exclusion.

## Notes

1 There is, of course, a wide literature on anhedonic feelings but this condition does not coincide exactly with numbness because numbness extends beyond the incapacity of pleasure feelings. It is not apathy either because there are strong feelings constantly pushing against the metaphorical shield of indifference.

2 See for example another post in which the user writes: "Thank you for writing about the numbness, I've never heard anyone talk about that feeling on this site until you. It makes me feel less uncomfortable that it's just not me that experiences this and I just really appreciate it".

3 The anonymous excerpts cited in first person are all retrieved from now on from: https://themighty.com/2017/07/when-depression-makes-me-numb-not-sad/.

4 As it concerns the use of and application of empathy in the phenomenological method, see: Englander (2014); Gallese (2003).

5 For Fink, world-belief is "the primal happening [Urgeschehen] of our transcendental existence" (Fink, 1988, 187), such that "existing-within-the-belief-in-the-world and believing oneself to be human are inextricably one and the same" [Im-Weltglauben-sein und im Selbst-glauben als Mensch sein sind untrennbar eins] (KS, 115/109, translation modified). Hence, rather than as the "natural attitude," Fink preferred to denote the mundane predicament of human existence as Weltbefangenheit, captivation in/by the world (see: Bruzina, 1995, 57–60; Cairns, 2010, 95). Human beings, as such, are imprisoned by ontic preoccupations.

6 See also on time and self Lohmar (2010) and Simeonov (2015). From the perspective of the coexistence of this threefold layer, phenomenology and physics are on the same continuum: from a static perspective matter is an association of atoms and the force that keeps them together is their valence bonds. Yet, we cannot observe matter only from the perspective of their bonds in just one moment in time, because the observation would be deceiving at best. As Levere writes "atoms cannot be studied in isolation, but as they react." (1985) As Heisenberg noticed "Matter produces the force of gravity and the force of gravity acts on matter." Matter is a field and a flow.

The field as Schroedinger remarks "tends to be fixed, but the force it radiates is un-predictable" or as Einstein later explained "matter radiates waves whose frequency depends on its own structure." Taking away the waves from the matter would make the description of the matter lacking, not seeing the matter and being focused only on the waves would make the description of the waves at best highly mysterious. It is impossible to draw a line of demarcation between the visible and invisible, the material and the becoming, the being and time, real and ideal, given and meaning. There is the elegant equation of the physics Pauli that proves the interconnection between the two, meaning and reality (Peat, 1921, 56, 14, 16). Consequently, genetic and static eyes are both necessary to understand the elusive nature of time and the concreteness of being that time describes.

7  The theoretical and practical application of the phenomenological method has pre-cisely the goal to reactivate meanings and their essence through a methodical navi-gation of these three egological layers of reality and through a rigorous analysis of the outcomes brought forth from each of their egoic shifts. For example, if we are working from a theoretical standpoint our natural ego compares different sources with each other and is lead to take the authority of these sources for granted, the same when we work in an empirical way and collect data from different interviews. Yet, when we decide to apply the phenomenological method, either on theoretical sources or on practical data, our transcendental and practical egos come to play. The natural attitude of the psychological ego is questioned by the psychological ego itself which decides (practical ego) to apply the epoche in order to gauge the sense of the sources (if we apply the theoretical phenomenological method) or the meaning of the data (if we apply the empirical phenomenological method). In this shift the *ego that makes the decision* to perform the epoche, that is the practical ego, helps the other two egoic layers to gain a more rigorous and meaningful understanding of the data which will lead to a consequent reactivation of the sense implied in the analysis of that lived-experience (whether it was theoretically or empirically analyzed).

8  On this point read Hauskeller's argument (2012) in relation to the irrationality of emotionless arguments in bioethics and his article against Giubilini & Minerva (2013) where Giubilini defends the right to infanticide based on rational utilitairan bases.

9  Holoprosencephaly (HPE) is a birth defect that occurs during the first few weeks of intrauterine life. HPE is a disorder in which the fetal brain does not grow forward and divide as it is supposed to during early pregnancy (incomplete cleavage of the em-bryonic forebrain/failure of the prosencephalon to cleave into the cerebral and lateral hemispheres). The most severe form of HPE is alobar, where the brain is not divided and there are severe abnormalities, including absence of the interhemispheric fissure; a single primitive ventricle; fused thalami; and absent third ventricle, olfactory bulbs and tracts and optic tracts.

10  Percutaneous endoscopic gastrostomy (or PEG) is an endoscopic medical procedure in which a tube (PEG tube) is passed into a patient's stomach through the abdominal wall, most commonly to provide a means of feeding when oral intake is not adequate". Retrieved from Kennedy Krieger Institute.

11  Such as: intellectual functioning (Baumeister et al., 2002), increased aggressiveness (Buckley et al., 2004; Twenge et al., 2001), reduced willingness to self-regulate (Baumeister et al., 2005), decreased helpfulness (Twenge et al., 2007), and increased likelihood of engaging in self-defeating behaviors such as procrastination and risk-taking (Twenge et al., 2001). A lack of stable relationships is associated with an in-creased incidence of psychopathology (Bloom et al., 1978) and a variety of negative health consequences (Cacioppo and Hawkley, 2003; Hawkley et al., 2003; see Uchino et al., 1996, for a review).

12  Available online, retrieved from: https://www.africancentreforcities.net/wp-content/uploads/2019/02/CSP_climate_drought-lessons_20190218.pdf.

# 4

# RESTLESSNESS

## The Case of Ulysses Syndrome

## Introduction

Why do we feel restless even when everything is going well? Why do we let down people who put their faith in us? What is it that wakes us up from within toward self-improvement and self-expression?

In this chapter I am going to answer these questions by discussing the notion of emotional restlessness in its negative and positive forms and investigate how this problem can benefit from scientific attention in the bioethical discourse.

Using philosophical sources, I will consider restlessness as the energy that best defines the *Geist*[1] (spirit/mind) in its becoming a subject. Nancy's interpretation of Hegel (2002) describes restlessness as the main characteristic of the spirit which accomplishes itself in the infinite affirmation of the negative, that is, in the infinite unfolding of that inner inexplicable concreteness that is not yet expressed. Levinas (1978 a, 1978b), too, considers restlessness as a form of ethical energy evoked by the proximity of the Other. According to Levinas, we are restless because we cannot rest when the Other is close to us. The sheer proximity of an alterity is a reason for us to be awake and to respond to its presence. This form of restlessness positively affects us and prompts us to become a subject, an aware center of action.

Yet, I believe that there is a form of tormented restlessness that exists when our habitual thinking is disrupted and we are moved away from the center of our own system. It is as if we are put outside of our own home. What Schutz calls displacement (1945), which occurs in cases of people who have lost their homes and cannot come back to them, generates a sort of inner turmoil that erodes the capability of these individuals to be responsive and responsible for their actions. Missing home, figurative or literally as in the case I will discuss later in the chapter, results in a core lack of responsibility because the individual can no longer be the subject of their own actions. The center of their actions, in fact, is not within themselves because their own home has been lost or was never there. Of course, this interpretation implies a complex notion of home, which I will discuss in more detail later in this chapter, and does not fully coincide with the physical place. Restlessness can grow ruthless if we are incapable of expressing our being, becoming the subject of our own actions, and being responsible for our own intentions. The way to quiet restlessness is to have a home where we can rest, where we know we can recharge before we start our quest again. If one cannot count on themselves and trust that, when the moment comes, they will stand up for themselves and express their own true essence—if that kind of safe home is missing—then the restlessness will become increasingly difficult to handle. Restlessness grows when the individual questions or denies their own wake-up call.

## An Introduction to the Case

In this chapter, I will discuss the case of newcomers who literally left their homes and are, accordingly, decentered from their own lives. I will emphasize how the particularism of the health systems might often be pernicious to the re-centering process that newcomers undertake when in a new country. Being unable to understand how to take care of their own bodies and incapable of being in charge of their well-being slows down or even stops the process of becoming subjects responsible for their own acts; accordingly, this process fosters chronic mental or physical problems that I described later in this chapter as the Ulysses Syndrome. In the case of Ulysses Syndrome, the last stage of integration, which is supposed to be characterized by contentment, is, in fact, often accompanied by chronic problems that impact the newcomer's well-being from a physical and psychological point of view. I believe that reflecting on collective intentionality (Searle, 1990, 1995), especially in its pre-reflective singular and collective layers (Zahavi, 2018; Salice & Miyazono, 2020), can shed light on the reasons why physical distress arises. The group identification in which immigrants represent themselves is, in fact, void of consistent intersubjective and interaffective contents (Fuchs, 2010). The expressive forms in which immigrants recognize themselves seem to adhere to empty inter-subjective and interaffective representations that, even though they match those of the hosting culture, do not fulfill the meanings craved by the new receiving culture. The noematic sense of these representations would be fulfilled if the continuity between the immigrant's pre-reflective self-awareness and the hosting culture's representation could be safely established (Sartre, 1957). In fact, the self-awareness emerging from inward observation of the immigrant's mental operations might encounter contents whose meanings are foreign to the observer because they exclusively belong to the hosting culture. Yet, those meanings are also part of the immigrants' lifeworld and are essential to their new integrated identity. The right blend of individual and collective intentions is necessary to express their identity; yet, any incongruence between the two prevents any re-centering process and makes their process of integration draining and pointless. Hence, it might happen that what was once familiar to the identity of the immigrant is no longer essential because it cannot be actively exerted in the new country. Vice versa, what was not essential before is now essential for them to exist and be part of the new community. Hence, the plural pre-reflective self-awareness, which we know is nonthematic, noninferential, and nonobservational, becomes, without control, the new singular awareness of the intentions/emotions/attitudes which are felt as necessary for becoming part of the new society, although they are often felt as empty or inauthentic. In the second part of this chapter, I will show how regaining control and responsibility in this interplay between singular and plural self-awareness can help the immigrant to assimilate without going through the backlash of Ulysses Syndrome.

## 4.1 The Challenges of Restlessness: An Overview

Restlessness is a common state of being that affects life in all its various expressions. Similar to anxiety, numbness, or narcissistic traits, which I have described in the previous chapters, restlessness can also be quite disruptive for the individual, the community to which they belong, and the environment that surrounds them. A restless person might feel less integrated within the community they belong to, they might act as if their actions do not impact their surroundings, and might live on half of their potential because most of their energies are consumed by this ongoing feeling of absence of peace. A restless nurse, teacher, or politician can make very disruptive choices for the good of our lives.

Yet, this is a very common state of being that can be associated with more serious disorders, although it tends to be considered endurable, much like how we view slight headaches. My thesis is that the negative form of restlessness is caused by the loss of one's home, which generates a disruption of the "thinking as usual" system. The restless person experiences a break from their original environment and is, accordingly, decentered with respect to their own system. People suffering from restlessness are guests of their own life; consequently, wherever they are they cannot feel at ease or right; they feel that something always has to change for them to be right. It is as if they live with an ongoing slight headache which does not let them be 100% healthy. Similar to the "narcissistic flu," the sense of restlessness stems from the lack of ground, in this case the familiar one, underneath one's feet. In the case of restlessness, this ground is the home, a concept that I am going to discuss in more depth in the next section.

Feeling restless puts us through a sense of inner turmoil that too often is taken care of by either ignoring it or through the use of medications, that is, via a scientistic approach in which science and not the human being districates the complex web of intentions that have led to that state of mind. As I will show through the case of Ulysses Syndrome, a scientistic approach that insists on medicalizing the individual is not always beneficial when tackling the problem. This is even truer when one considers the particularisms of national healthcare systems. Uprooted individuals who are obliged to leave their hometown or move frequently are more easily decentered from their own system of habitual thinking and more prone to feeling restless because taking care of themselves becomes an additional challenge that piles up on the other ones (e.g., learning a new language, finding the right job, adjusting to the cultural value of the new place, etc.). In the case of Ulysses Syndrome it becomes evident that the lack of a universal healthcare system is more likely to generate chronic health problems in individuals who are not given the tools to say what feeling good for them means and how to take responsibility for their own well-being. When lucky, these individuals simply must trust what the healthcare system of their new country wants them to do and hope it helps them to feel good—they live decentered from their own primary home system: their body. In the case of Ulysses Syndrome I am going to present later in the chapter, this generates a chronic sense of inexplicable disquiet and chronic illnesses.

### 4.1.1 Restlessness as an Infinite Affirmation

In philosophy restlessness has been considered the defining quality of the *Geist,* the mind or spirit itself. The ongoing vital force that brings to expression existence in all its mutable and multiform aspects is in itself restless. Yet, it is thanks to this restlessness that our intimate essence can come to expression, it is via this restlessness that we find our inner home and sense of peace. Hegel wrote, "Spirit is absolute restlessness" (Hegel, as cited in Nancy, 2002, 5) or, in different words, "absolute negativity and infinite affirmation" (1971, 13). Hegel uses the German verb *begreifen* ("to grasp," "to catch hold of," "to comprehend") in order to explain restlessness as this infinite work through which negativity—the pre-predicative being that is not yet expressed—leads the spirit to become itself. Negativity indicates that concrete sense that is not yet visible, it is that confused concreteness that has yet to come to expression. As Nancy (2002, p. 5) explains, the immanent world in which we live is finite but, at the same time, it shelters and reveals in itself the infinity of its spirit, which expresses itself through the work of negativity, that is, the restlessness of sense. It is in the restlessness of immanence, that the spirit of the world becomes what it is without seeing itself (as if it were for itself an exterior end) nor finding itself (as if it were a thing here or there), but it effectuates itself through living restlessness of its own concrete effectivity. In psychological terms, it is through restlessness that the individual becomes their own self, finds their home and their way of being—choosing their own vocation, embracing their own character, owning their own choices. "The subject is what it does, it is its acts, and its doing is the experience of the consciousness of the-negativity of substance" (Nancy, 2002, p. 5). It is through the *Aufhebung* (sublatum, overcome of—technical term here to indicate the ability to overcome something by including it) of its negativity that the subject becomes what it is by incorporating and acting on what it is not yet. In that sense the subject is infinite in living through the restlessness of the spirit of the world. As Hegel continues:

> Spirit is not an inert being, but on the contrary, absolutely Restless [unruhig: "troubled," "agitated,""restless"] being, pure activity, the negating or ideality of every fixed category of the abstractive intellect; not abstractly simple but, in its simplicity, at the same time a distinguishing of itself from itself; not an essence that is already finished and complete before its manifestation, hiding itself behind its appearances, but an essence which is truly actual only through the determinate forms of its necessary self-manifestation. (1971, section 378)

Restlessness seems to be the natural movement through which Being endlessly comes to manifestation. This movement negates any predicative fixation of human reasoning and embodies the expression of the true essence. Restlessness helps the energy of Being to be expressed against any pre-given mental explanation. It becomes truly actual only through self-manifestation. In psychological terms, it is that inner energy that brings a young student to choose their own career path independently of what their parents and teachers would expect from them. Or it is that discomfort that brings a human being to choose the sexual orientation in which to feel more at ease. Restlessness is that actual infinite movement that brings us home; it infinitely moves from what is not yet there, in Hegel's terms negativity, toward a true manifestation of being, of who we really are. It is the infinite affirmation of being, not according to the predicative categories of being that have already been created but by creating new ones in which we can finally feel at home with our congruent self. As Nancy writes, "it is restlessness of self, for itself, and uneasy about itself; and because 'it reveals itself as other, infinitely in the other" (2002, p. 25).

### 4.1.2 The Responsibility of Proximity

What is the structure of this energy? How does restlessness move forward transforming what is not there yet into Being? How does restlessness relate to the safe home in which we can rest and find peace?

Levinas answers these questions through the ethical structure of proximity. For example, he writes, "Proximity is not a simple coexistence but a restlessness" (Levinas 1978a, p. 121). Proximity, in fact, involves an obligation for us to be present and awake to what is close to us. He writes that "proximity indicates a restlessness that overwhelms the distance one might want to take from the immediacy" (Levinas, 1978a, p. 82). Life is proximity in the sense that life presents itself as a line of events toward which we react according to varying degrees of awareness. For Levinas, the subject is, at its core, essentially discordant because its nature is dynamic and ever changing. As we remarked with Hegel, the subject is its doings and acts. Hence, the concrete burden of existence that the subject is called to ontologically bear in its life is not connected to the abstract idea of existence but to its concrete energy through which it moves. The subject is restless because it lives or manifests itself through the incessant "recurrence" and "trauma" of being called to responsibility. The "Here I am!" is an incessant traumatic experience of the subject who comes into existence by being itself. The subject is unique because it is at odds with itself and continuously subjected to the imperative of bringing that oddness to resolution by moving it to the fore. The singularity of the individual does not point to the individual as a unity, but to the individual as restless because other than itself. As Levinas writes, "The other in the same determinative of subjectivity is the restlessness of the same disturbed by the Other" (1978b, 46–47). Subjectivity is never at rest with itself as far as it is alive because the most essential element of itself is constituted by restlessness. To be a subject is to find oneself again and again recurrently called to respond to the Other. "The necessity of fleeing," he writes, "is put in check by the impossibility of fleeing oneself (…) precisely the fact of being riveted to oneself, the radical impossibility of fleeing oneself to hide from oneself, the unalterably binding presence of the I to itself" (2003, p. 64). Restlessness cannot be escaped because we cannot escape ourselves. These moments of absence of peace or this enduring sense of disquiet are there to awaken us to become a subject and to find congruence with the non-predicative concrete self that has not yet come to existence but needs to be. "In nausea," he continues, "which amounts to an impossibility of being what one is—we are at the same time riveted to ourselves, enclosed in a tight circle that smothers" (2003, p. 66). We have the responsibility to infinitely be who we are, and restlessness is that call from home that reminds us to accomplish this responsibility.

As Husserl writes,

> It is necessary for the peace and prosperity of people that the property relationships are determined separately. These regulations have to be adapted to the nature and situation of the people in each case and generally adapt to them as they are in the whole.
>
> *(Husserl, 2004, 95)*[2]

Mere movement and sheer calm refer to the unchanged form. (Husserl, 1969, 299)[3]

Peace and rest can be achieved when individuals express their own characteristics and weave their relationship with the lifeworld according to these properties. Rest is achieved through awakening. Individuals are summoned to express their own characteristics according to their own nature and to find their home in these qualities. Yet, as Husserl pointed out in the lines mentioned above, without movement and in sheer calm no change can occur and the individual singularity that each subjectivity represents would not be able to come into existence. We need the tension between restlessness and rest, awakening and sleep, movement and stillness in order to be a subject and to get closer to home.

## 4.2 What is Home?

Home is a multilayered concept. It does not necessarily refer to the physical building where our abode exists; it can indicate the physical or psychological space where we feel safe and can find rest. During my practice as a counselor, I had the pleasure of meeting numerous clients whose international backgrounds were quite astonishing, many of them having grown up on multiple continents because of their parents' jobs. Some of them mentioned this as one of the main causes for their feeling uprooted and restless. Once, I met a woman who seemed to be particularly at peace with her international life. I asked her what home was for her. She replied that home for her was where her car was parked. We were in Basel at that time, so I asked where her car was at the moment. With a big smile she replied, my car is in London now. From there an interesting conversation developed.

Home is a very difficult concept to describe. The jurist Beale considers home as "the place to which a person intends to return when they are away from it" (Joseph H. Beale, 1935, p. 126).

> The home is the starting-point as well as the terminus. It is the null-point of the system of coordinates which we ascribe to the world in order to find our bearings in it. Geographically "home" means a certain spot on the surface of the earth. Where I happen to be is my "abode"; where I intend to stay is my "residence"; where I come from and whither I want to return is my "home." Yet home is not merely the homestead—my house, my room, my garden, my town—but everything it stands for.
>
> *(Schutz, 1945, p. 119).*

Home seems to be the terminus quo of our wandering in the world as well as a place of faith. We trust that we will be able to return to it and rest when we need a break from the world. Anyone who knocks on the door of our home, metaphorically or literally, as Levinas wrote, awakes us from our rest, invites us to respond to them, and to undertake a new journey outside. It is not recommendable to stay home for too long, to ignore the knocking on the door; the resting cycle has to be balanced if we do not want to start suffering from, so to speak, insomnia. Regularly, we need to leave our home to take care of ourselves, to provide for the things that both we and our home need. Yet, it is important to know that we have a home and that this trustworthy place is there for us. It makes our restlessness bearable while we are out in the world trying to become subjects and it fills our wandering with the meanings that speak to who we really are.

It is certain that without a home we can barely find rest. It is in that home, in fact, that we can build the sense of reality with which we filter what happens around us. If the home is not a safe and welcoming place, reality will not be so either. In literature, Don Quixote and Sancho Panzas succeeded in maintaining their belief in the reality of their world because they chose it as their home despite the discordant interruptions of their experience. The inner home is the space of truth from which we view the world and give meaning to it.

"Being homeless" equates to being out of one's own system of reference and being de-centered in relation to one's own self. While others go about their daily lives according to a customary pattern, the person missing home has no pattern or system of habits to which they can refer; what would normally guide the smallest habitual choices in life goes missing and has to be continuously rediscussed or questioned—a way of living that can be extremely draining and disorienting. For example, the ways in which one expresses love and gratitude toward another person or is polite in distressing situations are simple habitual practices that we have learnt in our home, our place of rest, that we put into practice out in the world. Yet, when the home is missing, either because it is not a place we can trust or it is a place we were forced to leave, we are decentered from our own system and, accordingly, everything needs to be questioned. This generates an unhealthy form of restlessness.

When we live a decentered life, what is accessible to the members of the in-group becomes unattainable for the outsiders, the decentered ones. While those who have a home can rely on a habitual scheme of expression, the "homeless" cannot. For the "homeless," any form of expression, no matter how small, is draining. Any chance of rest becomes impossible because it either comes from the imitation of those who actually are centered, or it feels uncertain and wrong because it is disconnected from one's own center. The "homeless" form of restlessness is absurd because it does not lead to the responsibility of the subject but to despair and even growing restlessness. When acting outside of your own center everything you do is disbalanced; you cannot own these kinds of acts because they do not feel completely yours. Losing one's system of reference is as disorienting as losing one's primary language. One can become fluent in a language, yet consistently feel insecure and uneasy with anything they try to say. With time you observe how others express themselves and imitate that confidence, but it takes time before you can feel yourself in that expression. To recover a language as a scheme of [4] expression, one must not only recover its vocabulary but be able to pray, curse, and love in it. To catch up with the members of the in-group who have their schemes of expression and can freely rely on their "thinking as usual" systems, it takes an enormous amount of targeted efforts. The restless acts of an in-group member show all the marks of habituality, automatism, and half-consciousness while the restless acts of the homeless are difficult to understand, at times rageful, and often obsessive.

### 4.2.1 A Short Example: Christina

Christina, a young client of mine in her late 20s, came to my office because she was feeling a little off with her life. To me, she seemed as if she was living her life at 60% of its potential. She did not have a space where she could rest. Even more worrisome, she did not want to find that space because resting prompted in her a profound sense of guilt and inadequacy. After having left the US (her home country) as soon as she could, she chose to live first in Hong Kong and then in Lucerne, where we met. Her father's job took her and her family to live in a different city every two years. Her sisters were on the spectrum, although to different degrees. As a result of the continuous changes of residence, the problems of raising the two sisters, and having a husband who was always away for work, her mother developed severe depression. Christina had a loving relationship with her mother and wanted to help her with the family. She felt the responsibility for the family's survival and carried the weight of that responsibility on her shoulders. Yet, as soon as she reached the proper age, she applied to study abroad. Her mother was very encouraging; she did not want Christina to make the same mistakes she did. As a very responsible and mature kid, she earned a master's degree while providing for herself in her new, foreign environment. When we met, she told me that she was feeling very restless and miserable. She had commitment issues. Even buying furniture for her apartment or signing a two-year lease caused her distress. She did not have a home. She did not allow herself to have one. The home she left was a place of guilt and shame and the new home she was building for herself had to unconsciously look the same. She could not believe nor accept anything decent because, after all, she knew that her life was not her own but belonged to her sisters that still needed her help and to her parents who were left alone in despair.

Occasionally, she sought self-medication in alcohol which would silence the internal monologue of judgment and self-loathing. Using alcohol seemed to be a way for her to take from life what she was normally incapable of taking, that is, a sense of lightness and forgetfulness. Yet, she lamented the risk that her alcohol consumption involved. She was blacking out very often and putting herself in dangerous situations. She was desperately trying to delegate to alcohol her right to be happy because owning it herself meant betraying her home and her system.

What we did together was to rebuild her sense of home. I believe it was important for her to gain faith in a space that belonged entirely to her; a space in which she could feel safe and capable of exploring who she was. Reconstructing her home and giving to it meanings and values that resonated with her character contributed to lessening her sense of restlessness and to transform it into a force more conducive to her own self-exploration and self-expression. It was an immense joy for me to see how all the people in her life made space for her once she decided to own her space in the world. After only two months of work together, she fell in love with a man. She found the courage to accept that love and to share the news with her parents—being that the first time her parents heard her speaking so seriously, they decided to give her the freedom and the space to remain in Europe without having to worry about them and her sisters.

## 4.2.2 Being Decentered from One's Own Well-Being

Our very first form of home is our body (Merleau-Ponty, 2012); its well-being and health are signs of harmony and stability for us. Against a dualistic way of perceiving the relationship between body and mind, we cannot have a balanced life if our body does not feel safe. Feeling powerless to provide the care our body needs is like being forced from our own home. According to the place in which you live and the traditions by which you abide, well-being has different meanings and ways of being achieved. Having to learn these ways can be a tiresome endeavor when new to a country.

In cases of immigrants, asylum seekers, or expatriates who must frequently move from place to place, they can find themselves investing a large amount of energy in this process. At this important crossroads between psychology, philosophy, and medicine, even a privileged person might perceive that the mountain is too high to climb and they might start neglecting their well-being or moving the responsibility of their well-being to third parties. Given the amount of changes that a newcomer already has to deal with when integrating into a new society, learning how the health system in their new country works and how to appropriately take care of their physical and mental well-being can be seen as an enormous, almost futile, task. While I do believe that a nation's healthcare system is an important tool for feeling at home in one's own body, it is often one of the main reasons why people become decentered from their own home-system.

They might feel as if they have to step back from the care they can provide for themselves because they have to learn how to speak in this new language and trust that this new language will help them to express themselves and their well-being. Francis Omaswa said that health is made in the home, while hospitals are for repairs (Stefan Peterson, UNICEF Health Programs cited in George et al., 2019, ii137). Although health policies and systems around the world increasingly emphasize equity and inclusivity, certain vulnerable populations remain underrepresented, especially those at the intersections of multiple forms of marginalization and structural oppressions (Kapilashrami & Hankivsky, 2018). Rather than objectifying vulnerable groups in isolation from their social context, intersectional causes of inequality must be addressed by the health system (Larson et al., 2016). It is important to ensure that all people are at the center of the health system that contributes to their well-being.

I believe that Health Systems for All in the Sustainable Development Goal Era (Asha, 2019) points to the direction we should go to help improve individuals' well-being. A key aim of this program is to strengthen health systems by combining socially relevant science with effective, accountable, and inclusive institutions in order to guide diverse social actors on their path to health and equity. Everyone counts, but if one does not have the words to express their own worth, their voice becomes a burden more than a tool for collective social well-being.

It would be helpful to explore the contested and fluid boundaries of multiple social identities and networks that make up communities and provide a universal health system for these communities (Schneider, 2016; George et al., 2014). Schneider (2016) remark that embedded research that emphasizes engagement, listening, and co-production of knowledge with communities is an important factor for understanding and collaboratively governing their connection with other health systems stakeholders to ensure health for all.

The harmful form of restlessness caused by the permanent loss of one's physical and/or psychological home can severely affect the quality of one's life as in the case of Ulysses Syndrome, which I will now discuss.

## 4.3 Grievance and Ulysses Syndrome

In what follows I am going to discuss the problem of Ulysses Syndrome (Achotegui, 2014) in relation to collective intentionality as an example of the consequences that negative restlessness can have on individuals. Ulysses Syndrome is a chronic illness affecting a growing number of newcomers. This syndrome especially influences the newcomer during the last stage of assimilation, which is supposed to be characterized by contentment, with chronic physical and psychological problems.

I believe that reflecting on collective intentionality (Searle, 1990, 1995), especially in its pre-reflective shared and collective layers (Zahavi, 2018; Salice & Miyazono, 2020) can shed light on the causes of the psychological and physical distress characterizing the Ulysses Syndrome. In the case of this syndrome, the expressive forms in which the newcomers recognize and express themselves seem to adhere to empty collective representations that, even though they match those of the hosting culture, do not fulfill the meanings craved by the new receiving culture.

The following sections will examine first the meaning of this syndrome and the way in which the migratory process disrupts the habitual thinking that builds the normative cultural patterns orienting one's actions. It will then show how the pre-reflective layer is constituted and how important this constitution is for building a sense of safe home from which to express personal feelings. I will use the lived-experience of grief as an example to describe how disruptive the in-congruence between pre-reflective (home) and collective (group-system) emotions can be. In sections five and six, I will introduce a distinction between collective and shared emotions in order to soothe the negative form of restlessness and to foster the newcomer's ability to transition from pre-reflective to reflective layer in a way that is congruent to their own emotions.

### 4.3.1 Ulysses' Journey

When Ulysses left Ithaca, little did he know that his home would be lost forever. After 20 years of traveling, he finally returned to Ithaca but was unable to recognize it. Mournfully he cried, "Alas! and now where on earth am I? What do I hear myself? (...) He believes himself to be in a strange country, a stranger among strangers" (Schutz, 1945, 106). Homer's psychology of nostoi (the home-coming journey) sheds light on the complexity of a long journey back home and the longing for a home that seems to have ceased to exist. Unfortunately, we do not know how Ulysses felt after a few months of his returning home. Did he truly feel at home? Or did he ever fancy going back to Scylla? We know that only Argo, his dog, recognized him and that everything around him felt different even if still the same.

As mentioned above, the notion of home for a person who is forced to leave it is extremely complex. Once left, it is almost impossible to return. Even if most things remain the same, that place has changed, both in the memories of the person who left and in the people who have changed during their absence. Without knowing it, the home, the physical place in which one felt at ease, has transformed into an emotional token.

> It is the same problem which Heraclitus visualized with his statement that we cannot bathe twice in the same river; which Bergson analyzed in his philosophy of the *duree;* which Kierkegaard described as the problem of "repetition"; which Peguy had in mind in saying that the road which leads from Paris to Chartres has a different aspect from the road which leads from Chartres to Paris; and it is the same problem which, in a somewhat distorted fashion, occupies G. H. Mead's *Philosophy of the Present.* The mere fact that we grow older, that novel experiences emerge continuously within our stream of thought, that previous experiences are permanently receiving additional interpretative meanings in the light of these supervenient experiences, which have, more or less, changed our state of mind—all these basic features of our mental life bar a recurrence of the same.
>
> *(Schutz, 1945, 115)*

As Schutz beautifully summarized in the lines cited above, the newcomer loses their home in the same way that we, at each moment, lose our present; the discriminant factor is the lack of awareness. Being that home is a physical, see-mingly immutable place, it is easier to get tricked into the idea of its immutability.

## 4.4 The Process of Assimilation

In his 1964 study, Gordon simplifies an immigrant's assimilation into a new country into three main steps: acculturation (in which the newcomer is shocked by their entrance into the new culture and tries to apprehend as much as possible), integration (in which the newcomer enters different levels of the society), and cultural intermarriage (in which the newcomer mingles with the hosting culture from a very personal and emotional point of view ). I believe that Ulysses Syndrome locates itself within the very last step of this journey: emotional assimilation.

According to Gordon, when a person leaves their home for a radical change, the transition is characterized by a standard process of cultural, structural, and marital assimilation. Gordon believes that this process of cultural assimilation is inevitable, and differences would tend to disappear (1964, 66) into a form of civic assimilation where a conflict of values and power fades into harmonic co-living. Contemporary experience often tells us otherwise (Alba & Nee, 1997, 2003; Rumbaut, 1997). Even after living for several years in the new country, some newcomers might feel as if they no longer have a place where they can feel at home. Either the home they left behind has changed or they have; the structures provided to them by the new home might have failed them in moments of acute distress and created a space for unresolved negative feelings. These feelings affect their health and lead to what Achotegui called the Ulysses Syndrome (2002). In what follows I will examine Ulysses Syndrome and propose to use collective intentionality, especially in what concerns the field of shared emotions and their habitualizations within shared values and institutions, to help those affected recover from this syndrome. Before discussing my argument, I will explain what is meant by Ulysses Syndrome.

### *4.4.1 Ulysses Syndrome*

This term was coined in 2002 by the psychiatrist Joseba Achotegui during a time in which Spain was witnessing a strong wave of immigration. His geographical location allowed him to observe a recurrent pattern in the suffering of the newcomers and to study the bodily, as well as emotional, similarities among these cases. He called Ulysses Syndrome the recurrence of health problems—such as chronic fatigue, migraines, nausea, shortness of breath, gastric and osteo-physical pains—which seemed to be often triggered by the emotional turmoil of not feeling at home. The sense of exclusion which often generates a deep form of vulnerability, constant sadness, or a feeling of isolation, leads to low self-esteem and a sense of stagnation. Moreover, the multiplicity and chronicity of these factors is increased by the lack of a healthy network of social support and the inappropriate intervention of the medical system in the host country. Today, Indigenous Linguistically and Culturally Competent Community Health Educators (ILCCCHEs) and Community Health Workers (CHW) are working in close collaboration with WHO to address this problem through prevention and education.

## 4.4.2 Ulysses Syndrome: A Case

What does it mean to be healthy? How can we feel at home in our body? As described in section II.1, the answer varies from place to place, with the definition of healthy and the ways of approaching medicine differing greatly depending on where one might currently live. For example, even within the same medical tradition, the strain of antibiotics one might use in England will be different from the one administered in Switzerland. Yet, the body of a person traveling from one place to another is expected to adjust to the new environment without particular thought invested in thinking what it means, personally, to feel good and how to achieve this feeling. If and when this adjustment falters, it is the person who fails, and it is often up to them to find a way to readjust in order to feel healthy again. The red flag of any given adjustment problem has to be ironed out for normality to be achieved again.

In Bali, for example, ethnomedicine is applied in the form of a daily practice of offerings to the ancestors and protective spirits; these offerings are conceived as a way of maintaining a balanced relationship with the whole environment, including the unseen forces. A person who wants to fit in the working environment of any European capital, for example, might want to avoid sharing this worldview with anyone because it might be seen as foreign and eccentric. To continue the example above, this same person, feeling uncertain about the congruence between their own roots and the tradition of the hosting culture, would never question what kind of antibiotics she is taking to feel better and what feeling good means in the new country. She just tries, as much as she can, to adapt. Yet because of this urge to adapt, she becomes unable to listen to her body, to interpret its signals, and to feel the difference between how she does feel and how she believes she should. Her body, unencumbered by these concerns, does feel the difference and reacts accordingly. Because of this, she will become decentered from her own body. The incongruence between the pre-reflective layer of the lived-experience (what the newcomer unquestioningly experiences in the hosting country) and its intentional meaning constitution (the meanings that each experience has to acquire in order to be acceptable in the new home) often finds the body as a battlefield. Restlessness is the dominant mood prevailing over the others, but it is ignored in the same way that a slight headache might be. No signal sent from the body finds a space to be taken into consideration and listened to; yet, it is in our body, in fact, that we first live any incongruence. Instead of listening to one's own body, we are often encouraged to seek out immediate medicinal assistance. "Are you sad? Take this pill, and you will feel good." It is possible, though, that in one's own country there is no pill for feeling sad. There might just be some rest and more time spent with loved ones. The newcomer tends to ignore these small hints because they are moved by the strong desire to fit in.

On this precise point, Joseba Achotegui shared insightful descriptions of some of the cases he encountered during his years of practice; here for the sake of my argument, I will focus on a case of incongruent grief. This will help me to prepare the ground for my discussion on collective intentionality and shared emotions in cases of negative restlessness due to intense suffering.

The case of Eka, a Moluccan woman living in the Netherlands, is emblematic of this. Her father died on her wedding day. Shortly thereafter, she started having experiences that, within the Western biomedical approach, are perceived as olfactory hallucinations. She also became increasingly sad and withdrawn from social contacts. Her brother brought her to a psychiatrist who diagnosed her with depression and borderline psychosis. He proposed that she undergo a combined treatment of "talk therapy" and antipsychotic drugs. This only served to worsen her condition. She grew restless and unhappy. Besides the severe side effects of the drugs, her therapist tried to convince her that she had unresolved conflicts which further exacerbated her sadness. A couple of friends intervened and obtained funds to allow her to travel to her home country where she had an extensive social network with a clear understanding of her need for closure. Shortly thereafter, she recovered. Not only did her physical and mental symptoms disappear, but her overall well-being also improved. This outcome was possible thanks to the supportive conditions that were available to her.

This case shows how the problem was connected to the incongruence between what she was feeling and what portion of her feelings the hosting society was willing to see and accept. She was living decentered from her own system of existence. Adjusting to the new culture was taking away from her those lived experiences that made her who she was. Her grievance was incongruent with the emotions shared by the community immediately around her. In the long run, living so decentered from her physical and psychological home resulted in a detachment from reality because the intersubjective reality she was inhabiting did not make space for her intentions to be expressed and fulfilled. Her way of experiencing grief did not make sense in the new space-time of the hosting community. As Schutz remarks, "the pure we-relation refers merely to the formal structure of social relationships based upon community of space and time" (Schutz, 1945, 11). In her space and time, the we-relation of her community was failing her. She could not share her emotions in any collective intentionality. There was no way to share the sense of grief she was feeling for her father, neither in a physical way (obituary announcement, banquets, religious functions) nor in an emotional one (sharing memories with the people who knew him, seeing in the other her same pain). This particular example shows how paying attention to the structure of this problem can ameliorate the quality of life of newcomers.

## 4.5 Collective Intentionality

As mentioned above, one of the problems underlying Ulysses Syndrome is connected to intentionality and, in particular, the way in which an individual's intention blends into the collective intentions and emotions of the hosting society. Despite the different styles of assimilation, newcomers' adjustments might, ultimately, diverge in two dangerous directions that are equally high-risk for emotional incongruence: either newcomers align their intentions to the new customs and in so doing repress their own, or they push away the new costumes hence isolating themselves from the new community (Meszaros, 1961; Berry, 1976; Aponte & Van Deusen, 1981). In both cases they live a life that is completely decentered from their own system. In what follows I will show the importance of the distinction between shared and collective emotions, especially in what pertains to the assimilation process of one's own emotions within the collective emotions of the hosting society.

### 4.5.1 Intentionality of Emotions

Intentionality is a complex term that can be used as a physiological[5] and conceptual[6] guideline for understanding emotions as they impact the constitution of one's values and meanings. The word intentionality comes from the Greek *enteinein*, translated in Latin with *intendere* and in Arabic with *Ma qul* or *Ma na*, to express a general "aiming at" motion. For example, in Plato's *Cratylus*, intentionality is the directedness of consciousness toward its object described through the metaphor of an archer drawing a bow to aim an arrow at a target. In Stoic terminology, intentionality is *ennoemata*, that is, referential thoughts that connect the subject to its lived experience. So, intentionality is a *paron apon*, a present absence that connects the individual to the outside world according to the way in which they decide to constitute meanings. Thanks to the impulses from Brentano's (1874) and Husserl's studies (1900), the notion of intentionality as "objectual in-existence"[7] and "tension toward"[8] was brought back to the attention of a wide variety of disciplines: biology, neurology, economics, philosophy, and politics. Husserl's volumes on intersubjectivity (Hua XVIII-XV) and Stein's (1922) study on collective emotions opened the dialogue on how an individual's intentions and emotions are expressed and recognized in the collective society. Searle's 1990 paper "Collective Intentions and Actions" represents the birth of this notion which elucidates how individuals' intentions and, accordingly, their lived-experience engage with the lifeworld not only in an individual but also a collective way. The collective intention that describes the connecting bridge between individuals and their shared world should not be seen as a summation of individual intentionality and reciprocal attitudes, but as irreducibly collective (cf. Searle 1995: 27). I believe that this irreducibility contains important information for understanding and curing Ulysses Syndrome. In fact, people suffering from this syndrome tend to have their emotions disappear in this irreducible compound.

According to Stein's account of communal experiences (Gemeinschaftserlebnisse) "the relation between individual and communal experiences is constitution, not summation" (1922, 122). In our society, we encounter ourselves and the Other, often in a pre-reflective attitude, and engage with the Other in a pre-reflective constitution of collective meanings and values. For example, our sense of kindness when helping a stranger across the street is pre-reflectively constituted in our collective intention. Of course, the way in which we express our intention to help greatly varies according to the normative patterns implied in that collective compound. If it is an old lady crossing the street in a southern town in Italy, you want to make sure to use the right pronoun to address her (you plural) and to help by offering your arm instead of touching her arm directly.

### 4.5.1.1 The Crisis of the Habitual Thinking as Usual

What Heidegger calls "the habits, customs, and publicness of everydayness" (Heidegger, GA 63, 103) represent the result and the starting point of this co-constituting framework of habitual meanings in which we are pre-reflectively engaged and where we encounter each other in the definition of what is appropriate or inappropriate, legitimate or illegitimate. When one lives in a place for a long time, there is a normative pattern of behaviors nurtured by the responses that are repeatedly given to the network of feelings, emotions, and sensations connected to certain areas of lived-experiences. As Schutz rightly remarks, for the newcomer these patterns are disrupted from the very beginning; the newcomer's epistemological and axiological orientation scheme has to be rebuilt.

> The discovery that things in his new surroundings look quite different from what he expected them to be at home is frequently the first shock to the stranger's confidence in the validity of his habitual "thinking as usual."
>
> *(Schutz, 1945, p. 99)*

From ordering food at the restaurant to dressing for a party, the effortless little actions that initially did not require any activity of meaning constitution become, in the new hosting society, a reason to shake the newcomer's self-confidence. The validity of the "habitual thinking as usual" is put in crisis from the very beginning and a new pre-reflective layer of collective intention needs to be formed and integrated with the previous one which refers to the different spatiotemporal area of their home. Missing this specific integration generates a form of tormented restlessness that is not often enough thematized and understood.

## 4.5.2 Pre-reflective Layer and Emotions

Biologist Freeman writes, "All actions are emotional, and at the same time they have their reasons and explanations. This is the nature of intentional behavior."[9] What moves the passive pre-reflective synthesis of data to active subjective engagement with the environment is the network of sensations, feelings, and emotions. For the newcomers to feel their personal passive layer as congruent with the collective one, it takes the stratification, through time, of new passive sensory data that motivate the individual to act in harmony with the hosting country. A new network of sensations, feelings, and emotions needs to form through time.

Strong intentionalism states that emotions have an axiological (Husserl, 1984) and hedonic (Colombetti, 2005) valence (positive, negative, or neutral[10]) which is, in a way, a reflective representation of the content of the experience. Literally, emotions (*e-movere*) are motivating (*motus*) movements. Deonna and Teroni[11] describe the intentionality of emotions as through and through because emotions are attitudes that we take in relation to objects provided by a cognitive base. "Each emotion consists in a specific felt bodily stance towards objects or situations, which is correct or incorrect as a function of whether or not these objects and situations exemplify the relevant evaluative property" (2012). Intentionality is not determined by a form of directionality that goes from the subject to the object or vice-versa (*concreta* to *abstracta*), because both directions are co-present. Intentionality accompanies the act; it is that with which the act constitutes itself in a particular form of time. As Husserl wrote there is no "ego as a relational center" (Hua XIX, LI V, 376; En. tr. 100) (12b), but there is the "I that lives in the act. (…) The idea of the ego may be specially ready to come to the fore, or rather to be recreated anew, but only when it is really so recreated, and built into our act, do we refer to the object in a manner to which something descriptively ostensible corresponds" (Hua XIX, LI V, 376, En. tr. 100). Emotional reality results from the ongoing co-presence and co-participation of the correlated subject and its object, noesis and noema, agent and its surrounding. The passivity of our vegetative state holds an important part of our intentionality whose responsibility we rarely claim and whose motivations and contents we rarely question because our subjectivity is not yet there. Nevertheless, this intentionality is equally responsible for the constitution of a pre-reflective layer that surrounds us and generates a sense of harmony we feel with the environment. The primordial and pre-reflective roots of this intentionality are very important in the incongruency of collective emotions. "Primordiality is a system of impulses" (E III 5, cit. in Paci 260-262) that, in a pre-reflective way, constitutes the reality of the individual before his ego-center and subjectivity is called into existence.

The newcomer is not aware of the new reality that is going to populate their passive world, yet this reality infiltrates their passive world at each moment, interacting with its motivational structure and emotions. It is in this early form of incongruence that liminal restlessness insidiates to awake the subject to repair the incongruence. The transition from egoless synthetic processes to egoic meaning-giving (Sinngebung) activity is characterized by the affections that sensations exert on the egoic core of the subject. To be effective, this transition needs to be authentic, which literally means that what is in transition from the egoless pre-reflective layer to the egoic reflective one has to be the same (from Greek autós, αὐτός). When this mobile core, which Husserl calls a volitional body (Hua Mat IV, 186), adjusts too quickly to external egoic meanings and values, there is a higher chance for the individual to develop emotional incongruence and negative restlessness. The newcomer's primal environment, that is, what surrounds this layer of affections and reactions of their primal form of the ego—the sphere of irritability, as Husserl calls it (Hua XXXIII, text 1)—needs to be synthesized in an authentic way. This represents the lowest level of affections from which the ego emerges and reacts to the irritating affecting matter by deciding what position it is going to take (Hua XXXIII, text 1, 5, 6, 9, 10). This is an important node of emotional congruence for producing authentic meaning and values in which the newcomers can recognize themselves.

### 4.5.2.1 Summation and Not Constitution

In the case of Ulysses Syndrome, the problem is that what is collectively constituted is summatively assembled and not co-constituted. In the newcomer's life, the pre-reflective, emotional, and affective layer combines, by nature, with that of the others' in a summative and not constitutive way because of the crisis of habitual thinking we mentioned above. In fact, the newcomer's subjective ego is not there yet, or, so to speak, is not awake to this pre-reflective layer. Since they are busy reconstituting the meaning and values of the smallest, yet necessary, lived-experiences to survive and adjust, their ego cannot constitute yet more complex meanings for their surroundings. Their volitional body can only accept or refuse what the passivity of their intentions proposes to them at each moment. This ego can only add or subtract itself to the meanings and values that have already been constituted in the host country. The change of the life of the newcomer is such that it inevitably impacts the passive layer of their intentions and, for a period of time, it prevents the constitutive core of their emotional life to constitute complex meanings and values that can feel congruent to the experience. It generates a summation of information and not yet a constitution of meanings. While the constitution of meanings would help the individual to regain their own center and express the energy of their passive syntheses toward meanings that feel close to themselves the summation is another variant of decentering. The individual, in fact, cannot be the subject of their own actions because they delegate the meanings of their own acts to the in-group members that form the collectivity to which they want to belong. In the case of Ulysses Syndrome, an improper form of collective intentionality occurs where the layer of collective emotions affecting the ego is incongruent with the previous, original one.

I believe that introducing a structural difference between sharing and collective emotions can create the space for correcting the incongruence as it stimulates the responsibility of the ego to own its pre-reflective layer of intention, constitutes meanings out of it, and shares it in the collective intention.

## 4.6 The Supra-Object of Collective Emotions

According to Stein, there is no explicit difference between shared and collective emotions. Emotional sharing indicates, in fact, life-coloring (Lebensfaerbung) (1922: 158 [190]) or a collective feeling (Gemeinfuele) that, so to speak, paces the "rhythm of a communal experience" (1917: 119 [100]). Emotional sharing originates in a we-subject that exerts its own intentionality (e.g., 1922: 113 [134f.], 115 [136], 117 [138]) through a sort of "individual subject" who may, "notwithstanding its distinctness and ineliminable solitariness, [become] a member of a supra-individual subject" (Glied eines überindividuellen Subjekts-, 1922:113). According to Stein, in emotional sharing, the individuals participating in the we-subject go through their own emotions as a plural subject. The plural subject is not a summation of individual subjects but is a constituting plural one that acquires its particular meaning from the mereological interaction of its parts and whole.

I believe that in the case of Ulysses Syndrome it is important to distinguish collective from shared emotions, especially considering the summative risk that collective emotions can involve. What seems problematic, in fact, is how the we-subject is constituted and whether all the subjects partaking in this constitution are equally represented. As mentioned before, it seems that the newcomer has a structural difficulty partaking in this constitution—because of the change of language, the bodily adjustments, the new working conditions, etc.—which results in the development of a potential incongruence between the pre-reflective experience of their ego and the we-subject. The volitional body of this ego tends to delegate the meanings and values constituted from the emotional collective experience to an external we-subject which eventually leads to losing touch with its own agency and meaning-making responsibility.

According to Stein, the intentionality of the we-subject (experiencer) can be fulfilled by a supra-object communally experienced in the feelings of the group. The group has its own emotional life-power or energy that aims at the realization of a shared goal. As Stein remarks, a person can feel an emotion that is shared by a group. When this emotion is fulfilled, the fulfillment is not expressed in first person singular but in the first person plural as a member of a group (1922: 116f) with the content of this fulfillment being a shared one. I believe that Ulysses Syndrome affects those people whose intentions are repeatedly not fulfilled by the supra-object.

### 4.6.1 Grievance in Collective and Shared Emotions

There is a difference between the supra-object and the constituted object which directly affects the distinction between collective and shared emotions. To explain the difference between supra and constituted objects we can use the example of grieving that served both Stein's and Scheler's arguments.

According to Stein, parents grieving the death of their children are both, seemingly, fulfilling the same emotions; there is no individual feeling there but a "we are grieving" (Stein, 1922: 116f). The content of their collective intention is a supra-object which fulfills the intentionality of the collective emotions that they are experiencing, that is, grieving.

> The father and the mother stand beside the dead body of a beloved child. They feel in common the "same" sorrow, the "same" anguish. It is not that A feels this sorrow and B feels it also, and moreover that they both know they are feeling it. No, it is a feeling-in-common. A's sorrow is in no way "objectual" for B here, as it is, e.g., for their friend C, who joins them, and commiserates "with them" or "upon their sorrow". On the contrary, they feel it together, in the sense that they feel and experience in common, not only the self-same value-situation, but also the same keenness of emotion in regard to it. The sorrow, as value-content, and the grief, as characterizing the functional relation thereto, are here one and identical. (Scheler, 2008: 12–13, translation modified) Certainly, I, the individual ego, am filled up with grief (over the loss of our member). But I feel myself not alone with it. Rather, I feel our grief. The experience is essentially coloured by the fact that others are partaking in it, or better, by the fact that I am partaking in it only as a member of a community. We are affected by the loss, and we grieve over it. And this "we" encompasses not only those who feel the grief as I do, but all those who are included in the group; even those who perhaps do not know of the event, and even the members of the group who lived earlier or will live later.
>
> *(Stein, 1922: 113f. [134]; see 117 [137])*

The problem for newcomers' emotional lives lies exactly in the fulfillment of this reflecting feeling. The constitution of the we-subject does not necessarily take place in the communion of intentions, hence they cannot generate contents that make sense to them. The supra-object is a meaningless or foreign object to them. To offer meaningful comfort to their grief, the correlate of their grief has to be a constituted object which holds a sense in which they can participate and recognize themselves.

In the story about the Moluccan woman grieving for her father, the fulfillment of the collective subject's intention was not doing justice to what the object of her intention demanded. Rather, the communal intention experiencer-experienced was taking room away from the genuineness of her grieving experience. Because of the space-time structure on which any we-relation is based (Schutz, 1945, 11), her grief was not one with the time and space of the other members of her family on the Moluccan islands nor with those around her in the Netherlands. Eka was decentered from her own system of meanings and values and struggled restlessly to be herself in her sense of grievance.

### 4.6.1.1 Fusion versus Sharing

According to Schmidt (2014, 9), shared feelings involve a phenomenological fusion in a straightforward sense. When parents are grieving for their child, "while both individuals experience a feeling of grief, there are not two feelings involved in this case, but only *one*. The parents' feeling of grief is *numerically identical*" (Schmidt, 2009, 69). According to Schmidt, "I can't really know how you feel," because my feeling *is* your feeling, or rather: my feeling isn't really mine, and yours isn't yours, but *ours*. Shared feelings are conscious experiences whose subjective aspect is not singular ('for me'), but plural ('for us')" (Schmid, 2014b: 9).

Differently from Schmidt and more in line with Szanto's account of shared emotions (2015), I believe that this fusion is truer for collective emotions than for shared emotions. For emotions to be shared, a subject has to be there and take responsibility for the network of passive data that its own feelings and sensations are producing. This subject has to decide what to share and what meanings and values to assign to these data. When successful, the experienced content of collective emotions is a supra-object deriving from contagious fusion and not the summation of we-intentions of the individuals partaking in those emotions. Yet, for the newcomers, as explained before, it is more natural to let themselves go with this fusion given their occurring crisis of habitual thinking. On the other hand, in shared emotions the sensorial-object which is correlated to a shared given emotion has sufficient structural space to do justice to what is experienced because it involves an egoic constituting activity. The pre-reflected layer of what that object is for the ego and for the environment to which the ego belongs remains as the basic layer of the intentional act but there is space for the ego to act through a sharing act toward collectivity. The intentional fulfillment of shared emotions has higher chances to be congruent to the emotion I am experiencing and on which I am reflecting while I am creating a meaning. The shared intention can be fulfilled if the "intention to realize the communal experience is fulfilled" and the intention "does justice" to "what the object demands" (Hatfield et al., 2014).

While Stein[12] and Schmidt seem to believe that a shared emotion can be fulfilled by a supra-object, I believe that an emotion is fully shared when its intentional correlate, the experienced, is a constituted content that does justice to what is given in the pre-reflective realm through the network of affections, sensations, and feelings. The supra-object is the intentional correlate of collective, not shared, emotions which emerges, at its best, as the correlate of the fusion of we-intentions.

While shared emotions involve the awakened ego to reflect on its pre-reflective layer as it emerges from the passive network of sensations, feelings, and emotions, collective emotions can remain empty on a pre-reflective layer and their reference can be fulfilled by a supra-object whose values and meanings do not resonate with the pre-reflective layer of the participants. There is no need for intentional reflection in collective emotions—parents are grieving and the spontaneity of that emotion is fulfilled automatically on a sensuous level. For shared emotions, instead, the ego has to take a position in relation to its pre-reflective content and make a meaning out of it—a woman needs to grieve her father's death in a meaningful way otherwise her passive life would create an alternate reality as an outlet for her strong emotions (olfactory hallucinations, for example).

As remarked by Schutz (1945), the newcomer has to confront the thinking as a usual system of habituation, hence everything has to be put in question every day, even more so their own emotions. Collective emotions cannot arise in a way that is consistent with the passivity of their experience because that experience is not yet habitual, which means that it takes more reflective effort to bring it to a meaning and value constitution level.

I think that introducing the distinction between collective and shared emotions is important for making room for expressing congruent emotions within a diverse community, especially in the early stages of assimilation in which patterns of habituations have yet to be established. It is, in fact, the incongruent content of collective emotions that might lead to a stratification of incongruent emotional contents and a consequent restlessness which impacts the newcomer's well-being. Keeping in mind the difference between shared and collective emotions can benefit the emotional balance of the newcomers.

### 4.6.1.2 A Short Reflection on the Normative Pattern of Emotions

In Ulysses Syndrome the emotional problem is originally triggered by the disruption of the habitual thinking that occurs once the newcomer arrives in the hosting society. The restlessness that this disruption triggers is often handled as a slight headache that needs to be endured. I believe that this "headache" needs to be taken more seriously because it can generate greater chronic pain. This disruption might, in fact, undermine the meaning-constitution activity that promotes the transition from the pre-reflective layer in which we feel at home into the reflective layers in which we constitute meanings that are to be used "outside" in the intersubjective reality. The individuals suffering from this disorder lose the connection with their physical and psychological homes and start living a decentered life in which the incongruence between their acts and who they are grows stronger and stranger. Their acts, in fact, are not subjective but intrinsically belong to a collectivity that the newcomers try to imitate. The newcomers are too busy rebuilding their system of thinking as usual to ponder the congruence of their feelings in relation to each expression of collective intention. The cultural pattern of the in-group members is no longer a subject matter of the newcomer's thought but a segment of the world that has to be dominated by action. The newcomer is a person that has to question everything, while the in-group member does not; it is as if the newcomer has lost authority on their own system of beliefs—accordingly on the pre-reflective layer sensations, feelings, emotions—because they do not partake in the vivid historical tradition by which it has been formed (Schutz, 1945, 97).

In the case of acute restlessness, the main structural problem is triggered by the sensorial object of emotions which does not elicit a subjective act of sharing from the individual. While in collective emotions there is a high risk that almost all the individual's pre-reflective realm is not brought into reflection because of the fusion occurring in the we-intentions and its fulfillment with the supra-object, shared emotions leave more space for the individuals to become responsible for their emotional sharing and for the transformation of the pre-reflective contents of their emotions into congruent meanings and values.

We can explain this point using Eka's example. In her case, despite the good intentions of the people around her, she was completely left alone in her grief. The sensorial object—in this case, the death of Eka's father—became a supra-thing in which she could not invest any genuine emotions; it was not a co-constituted object which represented a certain emotional and axiological meaning for her and the people around her. The collective web of emotions occurring in that specific spatiotemporal locus became an empty token that was preventing her volitional body from coming into contact with her own pre-reflective network of feelings and sensations and transforming that network into a meaning. She was living her life as a guest and not as a subject. The fulfillment of her intentional act was completed by a concreteness that was foreign to her: a supra-object congruent with foreign intentions. The immediate community around her took part in her feelings of mourning and in good faith created a space for these common feelings to be expressed; yet this collective emotional grief was not congruent to Eka's passive primordial feelings. That collective unity, then, caused her to need to find a new fulfillment for her emotional intentions, her depression, and, later on, her hallucinations. Yet, her olfactory hallucinations were explained by the hosting community not as emotional incongruence and need for integrity but as psychotic episodes (both emotional incongruence and the need for integrity present themselves through psychotic episodes because these deep needs could not find a way to be fulfilled); her feeling of deep sadness was connected to unresolved conflict within her family. The truth was that the sensory object, or the content of her grief, was not fulfilled by a content that felt congruent to her intentions.

For newcomers, it often happens that collective intentions and their consequent content, which is expressed in the supra-object, foster emotional incongruence rather than reinforcing their sense of integrity. The physical and geographical incongruence that is at the basis of the newcomer's life produces an ongoing constitution of passive contents that does not match the individual intentions. That is, Eka experienced the loss of her father, yet life went on around her. Even if her brother probably felt the same grief as her, the pre-reflective passive intention constituting the grief for their loss was made more difficult by being in a society that felt foreign to them. Small evocative gestures signaling grief and showing respect for it—for example, in Western societies it would be publishing an obituary, fasting, dressing in black—all that was missing for her. The pre-reflective contents that are muted in the passivity of life and the emotional sharing transformed itself into an incongruent collective emotion. Even Stein remarks that "the content of the individual experience can very closely approximate what is required by the supra-individual object, and yet by no means does it need to coincide with the content of the communal experience." Emotional habituation (Drummond, 2006, 13) can generate an emotional regulative pattern (Frijda, 1986) that keeps proposing misidentification and incongruence.

A way in which this incongruence can be attenuated is through the commitment expressed by the individual to normative patterns through time. Since the geographical distance cannot change and the newcomer is thrown into a new reality that might feel dystopian at times, it is important to educate the newcomers and the people around them on the quality of their demands in meeting the content of shared emotions. Building a safe home that they can trust and where they can rest to gather energy to become who they are—this is the goal of a good intervention. On this point, I think that Gilbert's account of shared emotions can be helpful for developing this form of education. Gilbert remarks, in fact, that when sharing emotions in a collective manner the individual must "have a standing to demand" or to "rebuke one another" for what "is not in the spirit of the collective emotion," which (normatively) "instructs" and "guides" the "public performance," including the adequacy of its display and the emotion's "expressive quality" (Gilbert, 2014: 23ff). Physicians, professional caregivers, and mental health personnel should be put in the position of understanding this demand and facilitate the display of expressive qualities that might be diluted or even erased in the normative pattern generated by emotional habituation. If one encounters difficulty in expressing their own emotions because the emotional culture around them prevents it in an active or passive way, then suppression or unhealthy self-regulation would necessarily follow and would contribute to feeling trapped in constrictive emotional patterns (Colombetti & Roberts, 2015). Exercising the commitment to emotional sharing and the emotional pattern can be a way to avoid incongruence (Helm, 2008, 17).

## Conclusion

In this chapter, I discussed positive and negative forms of restlessness. Described in philosophy as a form of inner energy that encourages us to become who we are, restlessness can also be a destructive force. Bioethics can help to limit the destructive aspect of restlessness by reinforcing individuals' sense of physical and psychological home through a more comprehensive health system and a deeper understanding of the causes of this restlessness.

When we lose our sense of home, restlessness can lead us to do things of which we are not proud, things which make us feel foreign from our real way of being. Missing that core, which can be the literal home in which we feel safe or that inner space that we can trust as the ultimate resource to be who we really are, decenters ourselves from our own system and from the system of life in which we live. Losing that center means losing our ability to be subject to our acts and to respond to what we do in front of others that summon us to action. When we lose control over our well-being and become trapped in the particularism of different health systems that tell us what is good for us without us having a say, recovering this center becomes even harder. For this reason, in the second part of the chapter I discussed the case of Eka, a Moluccan woman, who was living through a moment of intense distress and was "cured" in accordance to the hosting society's health system with medications that only intensified her problem. This case of Ulysses Syndrome shows how the loss of her home generated a series of problems in the intentional acts with which this woman expressed herself and her belongingness to the hosting culture. Here collective intentions were often incongruent with the concrete fulfillment she expected and needed to constitute her own meaning and value. Yet, since she was a newcomer, her system of "thinking as usual" was completely decentered from her core and she had to employ twice the energy to reconstruct it. She had not enough strength left to recalibrate the congruence between her own intentions and her responses in relation to the collective ones. To cure this negative restlessness which generated the chronic problems we labeled under the Ulysses Syndrome, it was necessary to bring congruence into her life so that she could find a home in which to feel safe. At the beginning of a migratory journey, it felt safer for her to blend into the collectivity and to trust that this collective compound would be able to produce the meanings she needed to survive. I believe this is part of the adaptive process and the desire to fit in. Yet, this behavior needed to be shifted toward a subjective responsibility of her own acts, meanings, and values in order to bring that congruence from which life could make sense. Fortunately, in the case of Eva, her home system understood the roots of her distress before her doctors could and did all that was possible to re-center her in her new system, creating a bridge between her old and new system which brought the congruence that was needed for her to feel at home, again.

## Notes

1  The translation of this word is very debated. In this case, we use the most common "spirit" as a direct translation for Hegel's use of Geist, although we need to consider that in English Geist could be also translated as mind.

2  Dass das Besitztum der Menschen gesondert, dass die Eigentumsverhältnisse bestimmt geregelt werden, das ist flir die Ruhe und das Gedeihen der Menschen notwendig. Diese Regelungen muessen sieh der Natur und der Lage der Menschen jeweils anpassen und passen sich ihnen im Allgemeinen ständig so an, wie sie im Ganzen Hua XXXVII, 95 (translation mine).

3  Bloße Bewegung und bloße Ruhe beziehen sich auf die unveränderte Gestalt. Hua XI, 299/.

4  Here I am borrowing words such as scheme or decentered from Merleau-Ponty (2012).

5  Jeannerod, M. (2006). *Motor Cognition*, Oxford University Press; Noe, A. (2004) *Action in Perception*, MIT Press.

6  Dennett, D. (1987). *The Intentional Stance*. Cambridge, The MIT Press

7  Brentano, F. (1874/2008). *Psychologie vom empirischen Standpunkt. Von der Klassifikation psychischer Phänomene*, A. Chrudzimski (ed.), Frankfurt, Ontos Verlag, 2008.

8  Husserl, E. (1901/1984). Husserliana, vol. XIX. *Logische Untersuchungen*. Zweiter Teil. Untersuchungen zur Phänomenologie und Theorie der Erkenntnis, U. Panzer (Éd.), Den Haag, Martinus Nijhoff, 1984; Zajonc R. B. (1980). 'Feeling and thinking: preferences need no inferences'. *Am. Psychol*. 35, 151–75.

9  Freeman W. (2000). "Emotion is essential to all intentional behaviors." In *Emotion, Development, and Self-organization: Dynamic Systems Approaches to Emotional Development*, Lewis M., Granic I., (eds). Cambridge: Cambridge University Press, 210.

10  Although Teroni and Deonna do not seem to consider the neutral valence of emotions (Routledge, 2014), I agree with Husserl (1984) in thinking that the adiaphoron is a third possible valence.

11  This problem is part of a long-standing debate concerning nonexistent objects and the problem of representation. Sparkled by Brentano's theory this problem invested thinkers such as Twardoski, Marty, Meinong, Frege, Husserl who approached a solution that tried to fill the gap between a definition of nonexistent objects as ideals and percepta. If you want to read more of my take on this debate, please see Ferrarello (2015).

12  If none of the members feels the appropriate grief, then one has to say that the loss is not correctly appreciated by the unit. If only one member has realized within herself the rationally required (vernunftmäßig gefordert) sense-content, then that no longer holds: for then the one is feeling "in the name of the unit," and in her the unit has satisfied the claim placed upon it (…) then, that which is intended in [by the others] came to fulfillment in the experience of this one alone. (1922: 115f. [136f.])

# CONCLUSION

"We don't have too much intellect and too little soul, but too little intellect in the matters of the soul" (Robert Musil, cited in introduction to *Agathe*, (2018) New York, NYRB, vii)

An important asymmetry is still present in our educational system—as Musil perfectly stated, we have too little intellect in the matters of the soul. Although a century separates us from his birth, our knowledge is still painfully lacking where it counts most. We need to improve our knowledge of emotions if we want to achieve sustainable well-being. In this book I compared common health problems to emotional ones in order to offer clear images to, so to speak, *see* the afflictions of our soul: problems like the narcissistic flu, the underlying headache of restlessness, and the numbness of sadness.

As mentioned in the introduction, I purposely chose to focus on problems that can chronically impede us from living fully meaningful lives because I believe that it is important to learn how to responsibly handle the problems by ourselves before they turn into more serious disorders. Unfortunately, today the trend is exactly the opposite. Emotional problems are mostly addressed by psychotherapy, which often is a post hoc therapeutic practice healing wounds that are already disruptive. The psychotherapist provides clients with skills that would help them to heal in the same way that a doctor provides their patients with medicine to recover from pneumonia. We know how to avoid pneumonia, yet, sadly, we do not know how to avoid depression. We know what pills help us to limit the damaging effects of depression but we do not always know how to repair our health from sudden dark feelings or how to know what signals show that our emotional health is in peril until it is too late. Hence, this book was written with the goal of reflecting on emotional problems so that we may learn how not to wound each other or ourselves, and how we may attain more sustainable well-being.

In comparing emotional and physical problems, it also becomes clear how difficult it is still for us to read the signs of our body and be there for our body when it is necessary. Let me use another bodily metaphor to explain my point. Let's suppose you feel a lump in your throat. You have the vague memory that you have already felt that way. Even if you are willing to pay attention to your body, you decide to interpret that organic signal as a sore throat because you are used to connecting problems in your throat to a common sore throat. Hence, you start taking menthol pills to heal it. Yet, the problem you were experiencing was not a sore throat but a reflux and the menthol pills made it worse. Deep down you knew that the quality of that pain was slightly different but you forgot what meaning was connected to that specific organic signal.

With emotions the dynamic is very similar but even more difficult to interpret because the signals from the organic body are less immediate. For example, if I feel very lonely and my partner does not seem to be able to understand me, I might be unaware of these feelings until I engage in a strange fight with my partner (sometimes not even the fight can be enough to point me to my sense of loneliness). Probably, the best way to go would be to rest, pay attention to the emotional wounds that are hurting in that moment, and, when I am ready, I might try to find the best channel to reopen a loving dialogue with myself and my partner. Yet, the common reaction to these feelings is suppression, rage, re-crimination, wallowing, etc.—all reactions that would just increase unhappiness and loneliness. The point is that we are not educated to train our interpretive memory of the organic signals produced by our feelings and our emotions. This education is not developed partly because emotions have a long history of being discarded as superfluous and disruptive, partly because we hardly train these interpretive skills in any meaningful way. We know when we feel hungry, sleepy, tired, and not much more. The optimal alignment of ourselves with our intentions that would increase our awareness in life and would make our well-being more feasible is somewhat externalized to professionals and mass-products that cannot always successfully take responsibility for meanings that originate from within ourselves. These professionals have the responsibility of interpreting more refined forms of meanings relating to our organic life; yet, in doing so, they encourage a form of individual irresponsibility for which the meaning-making process essential for one's own life is derogated to the psychotherapist's job—if and when the individual seeks aid. (i.e., I do not know how I am feeling. Generalized *Angst* is what I am experiencing; I hope my psychotherapist can tell me what this is about).

Bioethics is a discipline focused on the survival of the species according to responsibility and wisdom; I hope we can find in this discipline some space to focus on these burning problems. In agreement with the oncologist Rensselaer van Potter, the founder of bioethics, I do not believe that we can achieve well-being if we do not start from our inner peace of mind. We are implicitly trained to endure small emotional problems in the same way we endure a flu or a headache. Yet, similarly to when we have a flu or a headache, we do not want to behave irresponsibly and spread our flu to other people. Being responsible for our emotions would allow us to behave in a more civil way toward ourselves and others so that we may make better choices toward a common well-being.

Giving in to emotional numbness, restlessness, loneliness, or anxiety would make us worse living beings. We would become detached from our personal and interpersonal lives, careless toward our environment, and disinterested toward the consequences of our actions on ourselves, others, and the planet. Every careless and harmful action we take against our intimate and surrounding environment increases our distance from it thus generating psychological and physical harm. This distance, in fact, reinforces that same numbness that undermines our psychological and physical well-being. It is a tremendous vicious circle that bioethics in collaboration with other sciences can break. I hope this book can help the people who are animated by the best intentions to use these intentions for the best results. I believe that the goal of science is to find the flaw that binds us and prevents us from freeing our lives from bitter outcomes. Or, as Montale more beautifully expressed it: "Cerca la maglia rotta/ nella rete che ci stringe, tu balza fuori, fuggi!/Va, per te l'ho pregato,—ora la sete/mi sara lieve meno acre la ruggine" (Look for a flaw in the net that fetters us/You now. Break free! Jump out and burst/ Go, I've prayed for this for you—now my thirst/ will be easy less bitter the rust"; Montale, in Limine/Threshold—translation mine).

# REFERENCES

Achotegui, J. (2014). *The Ulysses Syndrome: The immigrant Syndrome with Chronic and Multiple Stress*. Retrieved from http://www.panelserver.net/laredatenea/documentos/alba.pdf.

Achotegui, Joseba (2014). *The Ulysses Syndrome: The immigrant Syndrome with Chronic and Multiple Stress*.

Alba, R., & Nee, V. (1997). Rethinking assimilation theory for a new era of immigration. *International Migration Review, 31*(4), 826–874.

Alba R., & Nee, V. (2003). *Remaking the American Mainstream: Assimilation and Contemporary Immigration*. Cambridge, MA: Harvard University Press.

Albrecht, G. (2005). 'Solastalgia': a new concept in health and identity. *PAN: Philosophy Activism Nature, 3*, 44–59.

Albrecht, G. (2010). Solastalgia and the Creation of New Ways of Living. In S. Pilgrim & J. Pretty (Eds.), *Nature and culture: rebuilding lost connections* (pp. 217–234). London: Earthscan.

Albrecht, G., Sartore, G., Connor, L., Higginbotham, N., Freeman, S., Kelly, B., Stain, H., Tonna, A., & Pollard, G. (2007). Solastalgia: the distress caused by environmental change. *Australasian Psychiatry, 15*, S95–S98.

Allgulander, C. (1994). Suicide and mortality patterns in anxiety neurosis and depressive neurosis. *Archives of General Psychiatry, 51*(9), 708–712.

American Psychiatric Association. (1994). *Diagnostic and Statistical Manual of Mental Disorders (DSM)*. Washington DC: American Psychiatric Association.

American Psychiatric Association. (2018). *Diagnostic and Statistical Manual of Mental Disorders*, (5th ed.). Washington, DC: American Psychiatric Association.

American Psychiatric Association. (2000a). *Diagnostic and Statistical Manual of Mental Disorders*, (4th ed.). Washington, DC: American Psychiatric Association.

American Psychiatric Association. (2000b). *Diagnostic and Statistical Manual of Mental Disorders* (4th ed., text rev.). Washington, DC: Author.

Anderson, B. (2006). Becoming and being hopeful: towards a theory of affect. *Environment and Planning D: Society and Space, 24*, 733–752.

Anderson, K. & Smith, S. (2001). Editorial: Emotional Geographies, *Transactions of the Institute of British Geographers, N. S, 26*(1): 7–10.

Apolinario-Hagen, J. A., & Vehreschild, V. (2016). E-mental health – "nice to have" or "mist have"? Exploring the attitudes towards e-mental health in the general population. *BMC Health Services Research, 16*(Suppl 3), 200, 0119:64.

Aponte, H. J., & Van Deusen, J. (1981). Structural family therapy. In A. S. Gurman & D. P. Knistkern (Eds.), *Handbook of family therapy* (pp. 310–360). New York.

Asch, D. A., Rader, D. J., & Merchant, R. M. (2015). Mining the social mediome. *Trends in Molecular Medicine, 21*(9), 528–529.

Baker, E. L. (1981). An hypnotherapeutic approach to enhance object relatedness in psychotic patients. *International Journal of Clinical and Experimental Hypnosis, 29,* 136–147.

Barlow, D. H. (2002). *Anxiety and its disorders: The nature and treatment of anxiety and panic* (2nd ed.). Guilford Press.

Bastek, T. K., Richardson D. K., Zupancic A. F., & Burns J. P. (2005). Prenatal consultation practices at the border of viability: a regional survey. *Pediatrics, 116,* 407–413.

Bates, D. W., Landman, A., & Levine, D. M. (2018). Health apps and health policy: what is needed? *Journal of the American Medical Association, 320,* 19.

Batson, C. D., & Moran, T. (1999). Empathy-induced altruism in a prisoner's dilemma. *European Journal of Social Psychology, 29*(7), 909–924.

Batson, C. D., Klein, T. R., Highberger, L., & Shaw, L. L. (1995). Immorality from empathy-induced altruism: when compassion and justice conflict. *Journal of Personality and Social Psychology, 68*(6), 1042–1054.

Baumeister, R. F., & Tice, D. M. (1990). Anxiety and social exclusion. *Journal of Social and Clinical Psychology, 9*(2), 165–195.

Baumeister, R. F., & Leary, M. R. (1995). The need to belong: Desire for interpersonal attachments as a fundamental human motivation. *Psychological Bulletin, 117*(3), 497–529.

Baumeister, R., Twenge, J., Nuss, C. (2002). Effects of social exclusion on cognitive processes: anticipated aloneness reduces intelligent thought. *Journal of personality and social psychology, 83,* 817–827.

Baumeister, R. F., DeWall, C. N., Ciarocco, N. J., & Twenge, J. M. (2005). Social exclusion impairs self-regulation. *Journal of Personality and Social Psychology, 88*(4), 589–604.

Beale, J. H. (1935). *A Treatise on the Conflict of Laws.* New York: Baker, Voorhis & Co.

Beck, A., Emery, G., & Greenberg, R. (1985). *Anxiety Disorders and Phobias. A Cognitive Perspective.* New York: Basic Books.

Berenbaum, H., Raghavan, C., Le, H.-N., Vernon, L. L., & Gomez, J. J. (2003). A taxonomy of emotional disturbances. *Clinical Psychology: Science and Practice, 10*(2), 206–226.

Bergman, J. Z., Westerman, J. W., Bergman, S. M., & Daly, J. P. (2013). Narcissism, materialism, and environmental ethics in business students. *Journal of Management Education, 38*(4), 489–510.

Berry, J. W. (1976). *Human ecology and cognitive style.* New York: Sage/Halsted/Wiley.

Bissell, D. (2009). Obdurate Pains, Transient Intensities: Affect and the Chronically Pained Body. *Environment and Planning A: Economy and Space, 41*(4), 911–928.

Bloom, B. L., Asher, S. J., & White, S. W. (1978). Marital disruption as a stressor: A review and analysis. *Psychological Bulletin, 85*(4), 867–894.

Bondi, L. (2005). Troubling Space, Making Space, Doing Space. *Group Analysis, 38*(1), 137–149.

Booth, R., & Rachman, S. (1992). The reduction of claustrophobia—I, *Behaviour Research and Therapy, 30*(3), 207–221.

Bouton, M. E., Mineka, S., & Barlow, D. H. (2001). A modern learning theory perspective on the etiology of panic disorder. *Psychological Review, 108*(1), 4–32.

Boynton, J. R., Danner, F., Menaspà, P., Peiffer, J. J., & Abbiss, C. R. (2019). Effects of environmental temperature on high-intensity intervals in well-trained cyclists. *International Journal of Sports Physiology and Performance, 14*(10), 1401–1407.

Bradley, J. J., & Kearney, A. J. (2009). Too strong to ever not be there': Place names and emotional geographies. *Social and Cultural Geography, 10*(1), 77–94.

Braun S., Aydin N., Frey D., & Peus C. (2017). Leader narcissism predicts malicious envy and supervisor-targeted counterproductive work behavior: evidence from field and experimental research. *Journal of Busines Ethics, 135*, 1–17.

Brentano, F. (1874/2008). Psychologie vom empirischen Standpunkt. Von der Klassifikation psychischer Phänomene (A. Chrudzimski, Ed.). Frankfurt, Ontos Verlag.

Brown, T. A., Chorpita, B. F., & Barlow, D. H. (1998). Structural relationships among dimensions of the DSM-IV anxiety and mood disorders and dimensions of negative affect, positive affect, and autonomic arousal. *Journal of Abnormal Psychology.*

Bruzina, R. (1995). *Edmund Husserl and Eugen Fink: Beginnings and Ends in Phenomenology, 1928–1938.* New Haven, London: Yale University Press.

Buckley, K. E., Winkel, R. E., & Leary, M. R. (2004). Reactions to acceptance and rejection: Effects of level and sequence of relational evaluation. *Journal of Experimental Social Psychology, 40*(1), 14–28.

Buckley, P., Hrouda, D., Friedman, L., Noffsinger, S., Resnick, P., & Camlin-Shingler, K. (2004). Insight and its relationship to violent behavior in patients with schizophrenia. *The American journal of psychiatry, 161*, 1712–1714.

Budd, L., & Adey, P. (2009). The software-simulated air- world: anticipatory code and affective aeromobilities. *Environment and Planning A, 41*, 13.

Burke, M., & Kraut, R. E. (2016). The relationship between Facebook use and well-being depends on communication type and tie strength, *Journal of Computer-Mediated Communication, 21*, 4.

Bush, G., Luu, P., & Posner, M. I. (2000). Cognitive and emotional influences in anterior cingulate cortex. *Trends in Cognitive Sciences, 4*, 215–222.

Bushman B. J., & Baumeister R. F. (1998). Threatened egotism, narcissism, self-esteem, and direct and displaced aggression: does self-love or self-hate lead to violence? *Journal of Personality and Social Psychology, 75*, 219–229.

Buss, D. M., & Chiodo, L. M. (1991). Narcissistic acts in everyday life. *Journal of Personality, 59*(2), 179–215.

Cacioppo, J., & Hawkley, L. (2003). Social Isolation and Health, with an Emphasis on Underlying Mechanisms. *Perspectives in Biology and Medicine, 46*, S39–S52.

Cairns, D. (2010) Nine fragments on psychological phenomenology, *Journal of Phenomenological Psychology, 41*, 1–27.

Callahan, A., & Inckle, K. (2012). Cybertherapy or psychobabble? A mixed methods study of online emotional support. *British Journal of Guidance & Counselling, 40*(3), 261–278.

Campbell, W. K. (1999). Narcissism and Romantic Attraction. *Journal of Personality and Social Psychology, 77*(6), 1254–1270.

Campbell, W. K., Rudich, E. A., & Sedikides, C. (2002). Narcissism, "self-esteem, and the positivity of self-views: two portraits of self-love". *Personality and Social Psychology Bulletin, 2(28(3))*, 358–368.

Campbell, W. K., Goodie, A. S., & Foster, J. D. (2004). Narcissism, overconfidence, and risk attitude. *Journal of Behavioral Decision Making, 17*, 297–311.

Campbell, Gaylon S., & Norman, John M. (2005). *An Introduction to environmental bioethics*. Switzerland: Springer.

Campbell, W. K., Brunell, A. B., & Finkel, E. J. (2006). Narcissism, interpersonal self-regulation, and romantic relationships: an agency model approach. In E. J. Finkel, K. D. Vohs (Eds.), *Self and Relationships: Connecting Intrapersonal and Interpersonal Processes* (pp. 57–83). New York: Guilford.

Campbell, W. K., Reeder, G. D., Sedikides, C., & Elliot, A. J. (2000). Narcissism and comparative self-enhancement strategies. *Journal of Research in Personality, 34*, 329–347.

Campbell, W. K., Hoffman, B. J., Campbell, S. M., & Marchisio, G. (2011). Narcissism in organizational contexts. *Human Resource Management Review, 21*, 268–284.

Campbell, W. K., Bonacci, A. M., Shelton, J., Exline, J. J., & Bushman, B. J., (2004). Psychological entitlement: interpersonal consequences and validation of a self-report measure. *Journal of Personality Assessment, 83*(1), 29–45.

Canu, W. H., Jameson, J. P., Steele, E. H., Denslow, M. (2017). Mountaintop Removal Coal Mining and Emergent Cases of Psychological Disorder in Kentucky. *Community Mental Health Journal, 53*, 802–810.

Catalano, J. S. (2010). *Reading Sartre*. Cambridge: Cambridge University Press.

Chaet, D. et al. (2017). Ethical Practice in Telehealth and Telemedicine, *Journal of General Internal Medicine, 32*, 1136–4.

Chorpita, B. F., Brown, T. A., & Barlow, D. H. (1998). Perceived control as a mediator of family environment in etiological models of childhood anxiety. *Behavior Therapy, 29*(3), 457–476.

Clark, D. M. (1986). A cognitive approach to panic. *Behaviour Research and Therapy, 24*, 461– 470.

Clark, D. M. (1988). A cognitive model of panic attacks. In S. Rachman & J. D. Maser (Eds.), *Panic: Psychological perspectives* (pp. 71–89).

Clark, D. M. (1996). Panic disorder: From theory to therapy. In P. M. Salkovskis (Ed.), *Frontiers of Cognitive Therapy* (pp. 318–344).

Clark, L. A., & Watson, D. (1991). Tripartite model of anxiety and depression: Psychometric evidence and taxonomic implications. *Journal of Abnormal Psychology, 100*(3), 316–336.

Clark, D. M., & Wells, A. (1995). A cognitive model of social phobia. In R. G. Heimberg, M. R. Liebowitz, D. A. Hope & F. R. Schneier (Eds.), *Social phobia: Diagnosis, assessment, and treatment* (pp. 163–184). New York: The Guilford Press.

Clark, P. A., Capuzzi, K., & Harrison, J. (2010). Telemedicine: medical, legal and ethical perspectives, *Medical Science Monitor, 16*(12), 261–272.

Clayton, S., Manning, C. M., Krygsman, K., & Speiser, M. (2017). *Mental Health and Our Changing Climate: Impacts,. Implications, and Guidance*. Washington, D. C. American Psychological Association, and ecoAmerica.

Cloke, P., Cook, I., Crang, P., Goodwin, M., Painter, J., & Philo, C. (2004). *Practising human geography*. London: Sage.

Cloke, P., Cook, I., Crang, P., Goodwin, M., Painter, J., & Philo, C. (2004). *Practising Human Geography*. London: Sage.

Colombetti, G. (2005). Appraising valence. *Journal of Consciousness Studies*, *12*(8–10), 103–126.

Colombetti, G., & Roberts, T. (2015). Extending the extended mind: The case for extended affectivity. *Philosophical Studies*, *172*(5), 1243–1263.

Colombetti, G., & Roberts, T. (2015). Extending the extended mind: the case for extended affectivity. *Philosophical Studies*, *172*, 1243–1263.

Cook, J. (2012). *The Scientific Guide to Global Warming Scepticism*. Available online.

Cook, J., Bedford, D., & Mandia S. (2014). Raising climate literacy through addressing misinformation: case studies in agnotology-based learning *Journal of Geoscience Education*, *62*, 296–306.

Cowpertwait, L., & Clarke, D. (2013). Effectiveness of web-based psychological interventions for depression: a meta-analysis. *International Journal of Mental Health and Addiction*, *11*(2), 247–268.

Craske, M. G., Glover, D., & DeCola, J. (1995). Predicted versus unpredicted panic attacks: Acute versus general distress. *Journal of Abnormal Psychology*, *104*(1), 214–223.

Damasio, A. (1995). *Descartes' Error: Emotion, Reason and the Human Brain*. London: Picador.

Dancy, C. (2018). *Don't Unplug*. New York: St. Martin's Press.

Davidson, J., & Smith, M. (2003). Bio-phobias/techno-phi- lias: virtual reality exposure as treatment for phobias of 'nature'. *Sociology of Health and Illness*, *25*, 644–661.

Davidson, J., & Smith, M. (2005). Emotional geographies. *International Encyclopedia of Human Geography*, *3*, 440–445.

Davidson, J., & Smith, M. (2009). Autistic autobiographies and more-than-human emotional geographies. *Environment and Planning: Society and Space*, *27*, 898–916.

De Choudhury, M., Counts, S., & Horvitz, E. (2013). *Predicting Postpartum Changes in Emotion and Behavior via Social Media*, Proceedings of the SIGCHI Conference on Human Factors in Computing Systems–CHI '13 (Paris: CHI), 3267–3276.

De Jong, C., Lucey, C. R., & Dudley, R. A. (2015). Incorporating a New Technology While Doing No Harm, Virtually. *Journal of the American Medical Association*, *314*(22), 2351–2352.

Demaerschalk, B. M., Miley, M. L., Kiernan, T. R., & Bentley, J. (2009). Stroke Telemedicine, *Mayo Clinic Proceedings*, *84*(1), 53–64.

DeMause, L. (1982). *Foundations of Psychohistory*. New York: Creative Books.

Deonna, J., & Teroni, F. (2012). *The emotions: A philosophical introduction*. London: Routledge.

DeWall, C. N., & Baumeister, R. F. (2006). Alone but feeling no pain: Effects of social exclusion on physical pain tolerance and pain threshold, affective forecasting, and interpersonal empathy. *Journal of Personality and Social Psychology*, *91*(1), 1–15.

DeWall, C. N., Baumeister, R. F., & Masicampo, E. J. (2009). Rejection: Resolving the paradox of emotional numbness after exclusion. In A. L. Vangelisti, (Ed.), *Advances in personal relationships. Feeling hurt in close relationships* (pp. 123–142). New York, NY, US: Cambridge University Press.

Diels, H., & Kranz W. (1952). *Die Fragmente der Vorsokratiker* (6th ed., 3 volumes). Dublin and Zürich: Weidmann. (cited as DK).

Donaldson-Pressman, S., & Pressman, R. M. (1994). *The Narcissistic Family: Diagnosis and Treatment*. New York: Lexington Books.

Douglas, M. (1993). *Purity and Danger: An Analysis of the Concepts of Pollution And Taboo*. London: Routledge.

Dowling, C. (2018). Change How You Feel: Change How You Breathe. *Psych Central*. Retrieved on March 1, 2020, from https://psychcentral.com/lib/change-how-you-feel-change-how-you-breathe/.

Drummond, J. (2006). Respect as a moral emotion: A phenomenological approach. *Husserl Studies*, *22*(1), 1–27.

Dyck, I. (2007). Emotional Geographies by Joyce Davidson, Liz Bondi, and Mick Smith, eds.. *Annals of the Association of American Geographers*, *97*, 448–451.

Efran, J. S., Lukens, M. D., & Lukens, R. J. (1990). *Language, structure, and change: Frameworks of meaning in psychotherapy*. New York: W W Norton & Co.

Eichstaedta, J. C. et al. (2018), Facebook Language Predicts Depression in Medical Records, *Proceedings of the National Academy of Sciences*, *115*(44), 11203–11208.

Eisenberger, N., Lieberman, M., & Kipling, W. (2003). Does rejection hurt? An fMRI study of social exclusion. *Science, 302*, 290–292.

Ekman, P., & Davidson, R. J. (Eds.). (1994). *Series in affective science. The nature of emotion: Fundamental questions*. Oxford: Oxford University Press.

Ekman, P., Friesen, W. V., & Ancoli, S. (1972). *Emotion in the Human Face*. New York, NY: Pergamon.

Emmons, R. A. (1987). Narcissism - theory and measurement. *Journal of Personality and Social Psychology*, 52, 11–17.

Englander, M. (2014). Empathy training from a phenomenological perspective. *Journal of Phenomenological Psychology*, *45*(1):5–26.

Fava, G. A., Grandi, S., Zielezny, M., Canestrari, R., & Morphy, M. A. (1994). Cognitive behavioral treatment of residual symptoms in primary major depressive disorder. *The American Journal of Psychiatry*, *151*(9):1295–1299.

Fell, J. P. (1966). *Emotion in the Thought of Sartre*. New York: Columbia University Press.

Fell, J. P. (1979). *Heidegger and Sartre: An Essay on Being and Place*. New York: Columbia University Press.

Ferrarello, (2015). *Husserl's ethics and practical intentionality*. London: Bloomsbury.

Ferrarello, S. (2016). *Husserl's Ethics and Practical Intentionality*. London/New York: Bloomsbury.

Ferrarello, S. (2018). Husserl's ethics and psychiatry. In M. Englander (Ed.), *Phenomenology and the Social Context of Psychiatry*. London/New York: Bloomsbury.

Ferrarello, S. (2019a). On the arising of the I in Husserl and Peirce. . In Ahti-Veikko Pietarinen, & Mohammad Shafiei (Eds.), *Peirce and Husserl: Mutual Insights on Logic, Mathematics and Cognition*. Holland: Springer.

Ferrarello, S. (2019b). *Phenomenology of Sex, Love and Intimate Relationships*. London/New York: Routledge.

Ferrarello, S. (2021). *Human Emotions and the Origins of Bioethics*, London: Routledge.

Ferrarello, S., & Zapien, N. (2018). *Ethical Experience: A Phenomenology*. London/New York: Bloomsbury.

Fink, E. (1970). Husserl's philosophy and contemporary criticism. In R. O. Elveton, (Ed.), The Phenomenology of Husserl. Chicago: Quadrangle, 73–147.

Fink, E. (1981). The problem of the phenomenology of Edmund Husserl (M. Harlan, Trans.). In W. McKenna, R. M. Harlan, & L. E. Winters (Eds.), *Apriori and World: European Contributions to Husserlian Phenomenology*. The Hague: Martinus Nijhoff.

Fink, Eugen (1988). *VI. Cartesianische Meditation. Teil 2*. Guy Van Kerckhoven (Ed.). Dordrecht: Kluwer.

Fleming, D. A., Edison, K. E., & Pak, H. (2009). Telehealth ethics. *Telemedicine and E-Health, 15*, 8, 797–803.

Foa, E. B., & Jaycox, L. H. (1999). Cognitive-behavioral theory and treatment of posttraumatic stress disorder. In Spiegel (Ed.), *Efficacy and Cost-effectiveness of Psychotherapy: Clinical Practice* (Vol 45, pp. 23–61). Washington, DC: American Psychiatric Association.

Frasier, N., & Jaeggi, R. (2018). *Capitalism: A Conversation in Critical Theory.* Cambridge: Polity Press.

Frederick, C., & McNeal, S. (1999). *Inner strength: Contemporary psychotherapy and hypnosis for Ego-strengthening.* Mahwah, New Jersey: Lawrence Erlbaum and Associates.

Freeman, W. (2000). Emotion is essential to all intentional behaviors. In M. Lewis, I. Granic, (Eds.), *Emotion, Development, and Self-organization: Dynamic Systems Approaches to Emotional Development.* Cambridge, Cambridge University Press.

Frijda, N. H. (1986). *Studies in Emotion and Social Interaction. The Emotions.* Cambridge: Cambridge University Press.

Friman, P. C., Hayes, S. C., Wilson, K. G. (1998). Why behavior analysts should study emotion: the example of anxiety. *Journal of Applied Behavior Analysis, 31*, 137–156.

Fuchs, T. (2010). Temporality and psychopathology. *Phenomenology and The Cognitive Sciences, 12*, 1–30.

Fuchs T., & De Jaegher H. (2009). Enactive Intersubjectivity: participatory sense-making and mutual incorporation. *Phenomenology and the Cognitive Sciences, 8*(4), 465–486.

Gabriel, M. T., Critelli, J. W., & Ee, J. S. (1994). Narcissistic illusions in self-evaluations of intelligence and attractiveness. *Journal of Personality, 62*, 143–155.

Galea, S., Nandi, A., & Vlahov, D. (2005). The epidemiology of posttraumatic stress disorder after disasters. *Epidemiologic Reviews, 27*, 78 –91.

Gallese V. (2003). The roots of empathy: The shared manifold hypothesis and the neural basis of intersubjectivity. *Psychopathology, 36*, 171–180.

Galway, L. P., Beery, T., Jones-Casey, K., & Tasala, K. (2019). Mapping the Solastalgia Literature: A Scoping Review Study. *International journal of environmental research and public health, 16*(15), 2662. https://doi.org/10.3390/ijerph16152662.

Gardner, W. L., Pickett, C. L., & Brewer, M. B. (2000). Social exclusion and selective memory: How the need to belong influences memory for social events. *Personality and Social Psychology Bulletin, 26*(4), 486–496.

Gendlin, E. T. (1996). *The Practicing Professional. Focusing-oriented Psychotherapy: A Manual of the Experiential Method.* New York: Guilford Press.

George, Asha (2019). Health Policy and Planning, 34(Supplement_2), November, ii6.

George, N., Parida, V., Lahti, T., & Wincent, J. (2014). A systematic literature review of entrepreneurial opportunity recognition: insights on influencing factors. *International Entrepreneurship and Management Journal*, 1–42.

George, A., Olivier, J., Glandon, D., Kapilashrami, A., & Gilson, L. (2019), Health systems for all in the SDG era: key reflections based on the Liverpool statement for the fifth global symposium on health systems research, *Health Policy and Planning, 34*(Supplement_2), November, ii135–ii138.

Gilbert, D., Gill, M., & Wilson, T. (2002). The future is now: temporal correction in affective forecasting. *Organizational Behavior and Human Decision Processes, 88*.

Gilbert, D. T., Pinel, E. C., Wilson, T. D., Blumberg, S. J., & Wheatley, T. P. (1998). Immune neglect: a source of durability bias in affective forecasting. *Journal of Personality and Social Psychology, 75*(3), 617–638.

Ginsberg, D., & Burke, M. (2017). *Hard questions: Is spending time on social media bad for us?* Facebook. https://about.fb.com/news/2017/12/hard-questions-is-spending-time-on-social-media-bad-for-us/.

Giubilini, A., & Minerva, F. (2013). After-birth abortion: why should the baby live?. *Journal of Medical Ethics*, 39, 261–263.

Gordon, Milton Myron. (1964). *Assimilation in American Life: The Role of Race, Religion, and National Origins.* New York: Oxford University Press.

Gosling, S. D., John, O. P., Craik, K. H., & Robins, R. W. (1998). Do people know how they behave? Self-reported act frequencies compared with on-line codings by observers. *Journal of Personality and Social Psychology*, 74, 1337–1349.

Gould, R. A., Buckminster, S., Pollack, M. H., Otto, M. W., & Yap, L. (1997). Cognitive-behavioral and pharmacological treatment for social phobia: a meta-analysis. *Clinical Psychology: Science and Practice*, 4(4), 291–306.

Greenberg, L. S., & Safran, J. D. (1987). *The Guilford clinical psychology and psychotherapy series. Emotion in psychotherapy: Affect, cognition, and the process of change.* New York: Guilford Press.

Gross, J. J., & Levenson, R. W. (1997). Hiding feelings: the acute effects of inhibiting negative and positive emotion. *Journal of Abnormal Psychology*, 106(1), 95–103.

Hamilton, C. (2010). *Requiem for a Species: Why We Resist The Truth About Climate Change.* Crows Nest, Australia: Allan and Unwin.

Hardin, G. (1968). The Tragedy of the Commons. *Science. 162*(3859), 1243–1248

Harrison, H. (2008). The offer they can't refuse: parents and perinatal treatment decisions. *Seminars in Fetal & Neonatal Medicine*, 13, 329–334.

Hatfield, E., Carpenter, M., & Rapson, R. L. (2014). Emotional contagion as a precursor to collective emotion. In C. von Scheve & M. Salmela (Eds.), Collective emotions (pp. 108–122). Oxford: Oxford University Press.

Hauskeller, M. (2012). Reflections from a troubled stream. Giubilini and Minerva on 'After-Birth Abortion'. *Hastings Center Report*, 42(4),17–20.

Hawkley, L. C., Burleson, M. H., Berntson, G. G., & Cacioppo, J. T. (2003). Loneliness in everyday life: cardiovascular activity, psychosocial context, and health behaviors. *Journal of Personality and Social Psychology*, 85(1), 105–120.

Hayes, S. C. (2005). Eleven rules for a more successful clinical psychology. *Journal of Clinical Psychology*, 61, 1055–1060.

Hayes, S. C., Strosahl, K. D., Wilson, K. G. (1999). *Acceptance and Commitment Therapy: An Experiential Approach to Behavior Change.* New York: Guilford Press.

Hegel, W. G. (1971). Philosophy of Mind. Being Part Three of the Encyclopaedia of the Philosophical Sciences (1830), trans. W. Wallace, together with the Zusätze in Boumann's text (1845), trans. A.V. Miller, Oxford: Clarendon Press.

Helm, B. (2008). Plural agents. *Noûs*, 42(1), 17–49.

Herman, B. H., & Panksepp, J. (1978). Effects of morphine and naloxone on separation distress and approach attachment: Evidence for opiate mediation of social affect. *Pharmacology, Biochemistry and Behavior*, 9(2), 213–220.

Hirschfeld, L. A. (1996). *Learning, development, and conceptual change. Race in the making: Cognition, culture, and the child's construction of human kinds.* The MIT Press.

Hogan, J., & Hogan, R. (2002). Leadership and sociopolitical intelligence. In R. E. Riggio & S. E. Murphy (Eds.), *Multiple intelligences and leadership* (Vol. 2002, pp. 75–88), *Mahwah*, NJ: Erlbaum, 2002.

Horton, R. S. (2011). On environmental sources of child narcissism: Are parents really to blame?. In C. T. Barry, P. K. Kerig, K. K. Stellwagen, & T. D. Barry (Eds.), *Narcissism and Machiavellianism in Youth: Implications for the Development of Adaptive and Maladaptive Behavior*. Washington, DC: American Psychological Association.

Horwitz, E. K. (2001). Language anxiety and achievement. *Annual Review of Applied Linguistics, 21*, 112–126.

Houghton, D. P. (2009). *Political Situations*. London: Routledge.

Huang, C. (2017). Time spent on social network sites and psychological well-being: a meta-analysis. *Cyberpsychology, Behavior, and Social Networking, 20*(6), 346–354.

Hulme, M. (2009). *Why We Disagree about Climate Change*. Cambridge: Cambridge University Press.

Husserl, E. (1923/1956). Husserliana vol. VII. *Erste Philosophie*. Erste Teil: Kritische Ideengeschichte (R. Boehm, Ed.). The Hague, Netherlands: Martinus Nijhoff.

Husserl, E. (1923/1959). Husserliana, vol. VIII. *Erste Philosophie* Zweiter Teil: Theorie der phänomenologischen Reduktion (R. Boehm, Ed.). The Hague, Netherland, Martinus Nijhoff.

Husserl, E. (1962). *Phaenomenologische Psychologie*. Dordrecht: Kluwer.

Husserl, E. (1918–1926/1966). Husserliana, vol. XI. *Analysen zur passiven Synthesis. Aus Vorlesungs- und Forschungsmanuskripten, 1918–1926* (M. Fleischer, Ed.). The Hague, Netherlands: Martinus Nijhoff.

Husserl, E. [1929] (1969). *Formal and transcendental logic* (D. Cairns, Trans.). The Hague: Martinus Nijhoff.

Husserl, E. (1970/1936). *Crisis of European Sciences and Transcendental Phenomenology* (D. Evanston, Carr, Ed.). Illinois: Northwestern Press.

Husserl, E. (1921–1928/1973). Husserliana, vol. XIV. *Zur Phänomenologie der Intersubjektivität. Texte aus dem Nachlass. Zweiter Teil. 1921–28* (I. Kern, Ed.). e Hague, Netherlands: Martinus Nijhoff.

Husserl, E. (1977). Husserliana vol. III-1. Ideen zu einer reinen Phänomenologie und phänomenologischen Philosophie (K. Schuhmann, Ed.). The Hague, Netherlands: Martinus Nijhoff.

Husserl, E. (1983). *Ideas Pertaining to a Pure Phenomenology and to a Phenomenological Philosophy*, First Book (F. Kersten, Ed.). The Hague: Martinus Nijhoff. (Husserliana III).

Husserl, E. (1901/1984). Husserliana, vol. XIX. *Logische Untersuchungen. Zweiter Teil. Untersuchungen zur Phänomenologie und Theorie der Erkenntnis* (U. Panzer, Ed.). Den Haag, Martinus Nijhoff, 1984.

Husserl, E. (1988). Husserliana XVII. Aufsätze und Vorträge. 1922–1937 (T. Nenon & H. R. Sepp, Eds.). The Hague, Netherlands: Kluwer Academic Publishers.

Husserl, E. (1908–1914/1988). Husserliana, vol. XXVIII. Vorlesungen über Ethik und Wertlehre (1908-14), (U. Melle, Ed.). Den Haag: Kluwer Academic Publishers.

Husserl, E. (1989). *Ideas Pertaining to a Pure Phenomenology and to a Phenomenological Philosophy*, Second Book (R. Rojcewicz & A. Schuwer, Trans.). Dordrecht: Kluwer Academic Publishers.

Husserl, E. (2001a). Husserliana vol. XXXIII Die Bernauer Manuskripte über das Zeitbewusstsein (1917/18), (von Rudolf Bernet und Dieter Lohmar, Eds.).

Husserl, E. (2001b). *Logical Investigations* (J. N. Findlay, Trans., and D. Moran, Ed.). London and New York: Routledge.

Husserl, E. (2001c). *Analyses Concerning Passive and Active Syntheses: Lectures on Transcendental Logic* (A. J. Steinbock, Trans.). Dordrecht: Kluwer.

Husserl, E. (1921–1926/2001d). Husserliana, vol. XXXI. *Analyses Concerning Passive and Active Syntheses. Lectures on Transcendental Logic* (A. J. Steinbock, Trans.). Dordrecht, Kluwer.

Husserl, E. (1919/2002). Husserliana Material, IV. *Natur und Geist. Vorlesungen Sommersemester 1919* (M. Weiler, Ed.). Dordrecht, Kluwer.

Husserl, E. (2004). *Einleitung in die Ethik*, Dordrecht: Kluwer.

Husserl, E. (1916–1919/2012) Husserliana Material, vol.IX. *Einleitung in die Philosophie. Vorlesungen 1916–1919* (H. Jacobs, Ed.). Dordrecht, Springer

Husserl, E. (1908–1937/2014). Husserliana, vol. XLII. *Grenzprobleme der Phänomenologie. Analysen des Unbewusstseins und der Instinkte. Metaphysik. Späte Ethik* (Texte aus dem Nachlass 1908–37), (R. Sowa & T. Vongehr, Eds.). New York, Springer.

John, O. P., & Robins, R. W. (1994). Accuracy and bias in self-perception: Individual differences in self-enhancement and the role of narcissism. *Journal of Personality and Social Psychology, 66,* 206–219.

Johnson, S. (1994). *Character Styles.* New York: Norton.

Jones D. N., & Paulhus. D. L. (2014). Introducing the Short Dark Triad (SD3): a brief measure of dark personality traits. *Assessment, 21,* 28–41.

Jones R., Lasky B., Russell-Gale H., & Le Fevre M. (2004). Leadership and the development of dominant and countercultures: a narcissistic perspective. *Leadership & Organization Development Journal, 25,* 216–233.

Kapilashrami, A., & Hankivsky, O. (2018). Intersectionality and why it matters to global health. *The Lancet, 391,* 2589–2591. 10.1016/S0140-6736(18)31431-4.

Keenan, H. T., Doron, M. W., & Seyda, B. A. (2005). Comparison of mothers' and counselors' perceptions of predelivery counseling for extremely premature infants. *Pediatrics, 116,* 104–111.

Kennedy, T. M., & Ceballo, R. (2016). Emotionally numb: Desensitization to community violence exposure among urban youth. *Developmental Psychology, 52*(5), 778–789.

Kernberg, O. (1975). *Borderline Conditions and Pathological Narcissism.* New York, Jason Aronson.

Kernis, M. H., & Sun, C. (1994). Narcissism and reactions to interpersonal feedback. *Journal of Research in Personality,* 28, 4–13.

Kessler, R. C., Sonnega, A., Bromet, E., Hughes, M., & Nelson, C. B. (1995). Posttraumatic stress disorder in the National Comorbidity Survey. *Archives of General Psychiatry.*

Kets De Vries M. F. R., & Miller D. (1985). Narcissism and leadership – an object relations perspective. *Human Relations, 38,* 583–601

Kim, J. (2013). The characteristics and trends of environmental conflicts in South Korea: 1990–2011. *Korean Policy Studies Review, 22*(2), 259–281.

Kim Y., Kim H., Honda Y., Guo Y. L., Chen B. Y., Woo J. M., & Ebi K. L. (2016). Suicide and ambient temperature in East Asian countries: a time-stratified case-crossover analysis. *Environmental Health Perspective, 124,* 75–80.

Kivisto, Peter (2005). *Incorporating Diversity: Rethinking Assimilation in a Multicultural Age.* Boulder, Colorado: Paradigm Publishers.

Koch, A. S., & Terrell, T. D. (1991). Affective reactions of foreign language students to natural approach activities and teaching techniques. In E. K. Horwitz & D. J. Young (Eds.), *Language anxiety: From theory and research to classroom implications* (pp. 109–126). Englewood Cliffs, NJ: Prentice Hall.

Kohut, H. (1971). *The Analysis of the Self: A Systematic Approach to The Psychoanalytic Treatment of Narcissistic Personality Disorders* (Vol. 1), New York: International Universities Press.

Kohut, H. (1977). *The Restoration of the Self. Madison*, CT: International Universities Press.

Kohut, H. (1985). On courage (Early 1970's). In *Self psychology and the humanities: Reflections on a new psychoanalytic approach* (pp. 5–50). New York: W. W. Norton.

Kohut, H. (1987). *The Kohut Seminars on Self Psychology and Psychotherapy with Adolescents and Young Adults* (M. Elson, Ed.). New York, NY, US: W. W. Norton & Company.

Kristeva, J. (1982). *Powers of Horror: An Essay on Abjection*. New York: Columbia University Press.

Lantos, J. D. (2001). Hooked on Neonatology. *Health affairs, 20*, 233–240.

Larson, H. J., de Figueiredo, A., Xiahong, Z., Schulz, W. S., Verger, P., Johnston, I. G., Cook, A. R., & Jones, N. S. (2016). The State of Vaccine Confidence 2016: Global Insights Through a 67-Country Survey. *EBioMedicine, 12*, 295–301. https://doi.org/10.1016/j.ebiom.2016.08.042.

Lasch, C. (1979). *The Culture of Narcissism*. London: Norton & Co.

Lasswell, H. D. (1930). *Psychopathology and Politics*. New York: Free Press.

Leary, M. R. (1990). Responses to social exclusion: Social anxiety, jealousy, loneliness, depression, and low self-esteem. *Journal of Social and Clinical Psychology, 9*(2), 221–229.

Leary, M. R., & Springer, C. A. (2001). Hurt feelings: the neglected emotion. In R. M. Kowalski (Ed.), *Behaving Badly: Aversive Behaviors in Interpersonal Relationships* (pp. 151–175). American Psychological Association.

LeDoux, J. E. (1996). *The Emotional Brain: The Mysterious Underpinnings of Emotional Life*. New York: Simon & Schuster.

Lemaitre, B. (2016). *An Essay on Science and Narcissism: How Do High-ego Personalities Drive Research in Life Sciences?* Autoedition: Lausanne.

Lemaitre, B. (2017). Science, narcissism and the quest for visibility. *The FEBS Journal, 284*, 875–882.

Leon, A. C., Portera, L., & Weissman, M. M. (1995). The social costs of anxiety disorders. *The British Journal of Psychiatry, 166*(Suppl 27), 19–22.

Levere, T. H. (1985). *Transforming Matter*. Baltimore: The John Hopkins University Press.

Levinas, (1984). *Transcendance et Intelligibilité*. Geneva: Éditions Labor et Fides.

Levinas, E. (1978a). Existence and Existents (Alphonso Lingis, Trans.). The Hague: Martinus Nijhoff.

Levinas, E. (1978b). *Otherwise than Being or Beyond Essence* (Alphonso Lingis, Trans.). Dordrecht: Kluwer Academic Publishers.

Levinas, E. (2003). *On Escape*. Stanford: Stanford University Press.

Lewandowsky, S., Risbey, J. S., & Oreskes, N. (2016). The 'pause' in global warming: turning a routine fluctuation into a problem for science. *Bulletin of the American Meteorological Society, 97*, 723–733.

Lewandowsky, S., Cook, J., Oberauer, K., & Marriott, M. (2013). Recursive fury: Conspiracist ideation in the blogosphere in response to research on conspiracist ideation. *Frontiers in Psychology, 4*, 73.

Lewin, K. (1935). *A Dynamic Theory of Personality*. New York, NY: McGraw-Hill.

Livio, Tito, (1975). *Ab Urbe condita libri*. Roma: Newton & Compton.

Lo, I. (2018). Retrieved from: https://www.psychologytoday.com/us/blog/living-emotional-intensity/201805/feeling-intensely-the-wounds-being-too-much.

Lohmar, D. (2010). *On Time. New Contributions to the Husserlian Phenomenology of Time.* Dordrecht-Boston-London: Springer.

Lorenzoni, I., Pidgeon, N. F., & O'Connor, R. E. (Eds.). (2005). Dangerous climate change: the role for risk research. *Risk Analysis, 25*(6):1387–1398.

Lovell, K., Marks, I. M., Noshirvani, H., Thrasher, S., & Livanou, M. (2001). Do cognitive and exposure treatments improve various PTSD symptoms differently? A randomized controlled trial. *Behavioural and Cognitive Psychotherapy, 29*(1), 107–112.

Lowen, A. (1983). *Narcissism.* London: Collier Macmillan.

Lupton, D., Maslen, S. (2017). Telemedicine and the senses: a review. *Sociology of Health and Illness, 39*, 1557–1571.

Luxton, D. D., June, J. J., & Fairall, J. M. (2012). Social media and suicide: a public health perspective. *American Journal of Public Health, 102*, 195–200.

Maccoby, M. (2000). Narcissistic leaders – the incredible pros, the inevitable cons. *Harvard Business Review, 78*, 69–77.

MacDonald, G., & Leary, M. R. (2005). Why does social exclusion hurt? The relationship between social and physical pain. *Psychological Bulletin, 131*(2), 202–223.

MacIntyre, P. D., & Gardner, R. C. (1991). Investigating language class anxiety using the focused essay technique. *Modern Language Journal, 75*(2), 296–304.

Mahler, M. (1968). *On Human Symbiosis and the Vicissitudes of Individuation.* New York: International Universities Press.

Marks, I. M. (1969). *Fears and phobias.* Academic Press.

Marks, I., Lovell, K., Noshirvani, H., Livanou, M., & Thrasher, S. (1998). Treatment of posttraumatic stress disorder by exposure and/or cognitive restructuring: a controlled study. *Archives of General Psychiatry, 55*(4), 317–325.

Massion, A. O., Warshaw, M. G., & Keller, M. B. (1993). Quality of life and psychiatric morbidity in panic disorder and generalized anxiety disorder. *The American Journal of Psychiatry.*

Masson-Delmotte, V., Zhai, P., Pörtner, H.-O., Roberts, D., Skea, J., Shukla, P. R., Pirani, A., Moufouma-Okia, W., Péan, C., Pidcock, R., et al., (Eds.). (2018). IPCC. Summary for Policymakers. In *Global Warming of 1.5 °C. An IPCC Special Report on the Impacts of Global Warming of 1.5 °C above Pre-Industrial Levels and Related Global Greenhouse Gas Emission Pathways, in the Context of Strengthening the Global Response to the Threat of Climate Change, Sustainable Development, and Efforts to Eradicate Poverty.* Geneva: Switzerland: World Meteorological Organization, 2018.

McCormack D. (2003). An event of geographical ethics in spaces of affect. *Transactions of the Institute of British Geographers, 28*, 488–507.

McLean J. (2007). Psychotherapy with a narcissistic patient using Kohut's self psychology model. *Psychiatry (Edgmont).*

McNeal, S. (2003). A character in search of character: Narcissistic personality disorder and ego state therapy. *American Journal of Clinical Hypnosis, 45*, 233–234.

Mennin, D. S., Heimberg, R. G., Turk, C. L., & Fresco, D. M. (2002). Applying an emotion regulation framework to integrative approaches to generalized anxiety disorder. *Clinical Psychology: Science and Practice, 9*(1), 85–90.

Mennin, D., Turk, C., Heimberg, R., Cheryl, C. (2013). Regulation of emotion in generalized anxiety disorder. *Cognitive Therapy Across the Lifespan, 60*, 60–68.

Merleau-Ponty (2012). *Phenomenology of perception.* London: Routledge.

Miller, J. D., Campbell W. K., & Pilkonis P. A. (2007). Narcissistic personality disorder:

relations with distress and functional impairment. *Comprehensive Psychiatry*, *48*, 170–177.

Montale, E. (1981). *Limine (Threshold)* cited in Rebecca J. West, The Marginal Readings of the First Voice. In *Eugenio Montale: Poet on the Edge* (pp. 13–17), Harvard University Press.

Morf, C. C., & Rhodewalt, F. (2001). Unraveling the paradoxes of narcissism: a dynamic self-regulatory processing model. *Psychological Inquiry*, 12, 177–196.

Mowrer, O. H. (1947). On the dual nature of learning—a re-interpretation of "conditioning" and "problem-solving". *Harvard Educational Review*, 17, 102–148.

Murray-Jobsis, J. (1990a). Re-nurturing: forming positive sense of identity and bonding. In D. C. Hammond (Ed.), *Handbook of Hypnotic Suggestions and Metaphors*, 326–328. New York: W. W. Norton.

Murray-Jobsis, J. (1990b). Suggestions for creative self-mothering. In D. C. Hammond (Ed.), *Handbook of hypnotic suggestions and metaphors*. New York: W. W. Norton.

Murray-Jobsis, J. (1990c). Ego building. In D. C. Hammond (Ed.), *Handbook of hypnotic suggestions and metaphors* (pp. 136–139). New York: W. W. Norton.

Musiat, P., Goldstone, P., & Tarrier, N. (2014). Understanding the acceptability of e-mental health – attitudes and expectations towards computerised self-help treatments for mental health problems. *BMC Psychiatry*, *14*, 109.

Musil, R. (2018). *Agathe*. New York, NYRB.

Muslin, M. D., Hyman, L., Kohut, H. (1985). Beyond the pleasure principle: Contributions to psychoanalysis. Reppen J., editor. Beyond Freud eds. *A Study of Modern Psychoanalytic Theorists*. Hillsdale, NJ: Lawrence Erlbaum Associates, 203–229.

Nancy, J.-L. (1993). *The Birth to Presence*. Stanford: Stanford University Press.

Nancy, J.-L. (2002). *Hegel: The Restlessness of the Negative*. Minneapolis/London: University of Minnesota Press.

Narrow, W., Rae, D., Robins, L., & Regier, D. (2002). Revised prevalence estimates of mental disorders in the United States. *Archives of General Psychiatry*, *59*, 115–123.

Nelson, E., & Panksepp, J. (1998). Brain substrates of infant–mother attachment: contributions of opioids, oxytocin, and norepinephrine *Neuroscience & Biobehavioral Reviews*, *22*(3), 437–452.

Nhat Hanh, T. (1992). *A Joyful Path: Community, Transformation and Peace*, Paperback. Retrieved from: https://terebess.hu/zen/mesterek/Thich%20Nhat%20Hanh%20-%20Peace%20Is%20Every%20Step.pdf.

Nochomovitz, N., & Sharma, R. (2017). Is it time for a new medical specialty?. *Journal of the American Medical Association*, *319*(5), 2017–2018.

O'Boyle, E. H. Jr., Forsyth, D. R. Banks, G. C., & McDaniel, M. A. (2012). A meta-analysis of the Dark Triad and work behavior: A social exchange perspective. *Journal of Applied Psychology*, *97*(3), 557–579.

Orsillo, S. M., Roemer, L., Holowka, D. W. (2005). Acceptance-based behavioral therapies for anxiety. In S. M. Orsillo & L. Roemer. (Eds.), *Acceptance and Mindfulness-Based Approaches to Anxiety*, Series in Anxiety and Related Disorders. Boston, MA: Springer.

Ostrom, E. (1990). *Governing the Commons: The Evolution of Institutions for Collective Action*. Cambridge, UK: Cambridge University Press.

Ovid, (2005). *The Metamorphoses* (R. Squillace & F. Miller, Eds.). New York: Barnes & Noble.

Panksepp, J. (1998). *Series in Affective Science. Affective Neuroscience: The Foundations of Human and Animal Emotions.* Oxford: Oxford University Press.

Panksepp, J., Herman, B., Conner, R., Bishop, P., & Scott, J. P. (1978). The biology of social attachments: opiates alleviate separation distress. *Biological Psychyatry, 13*(5), 607–618.

Pannell, S. (2018 ). Framing the loss of solace: issues and challenges in researching indigenous compensation claims. *Anthropological Forum, 28,* 255–274.

Pannell, S. (2018). Framing the loss of solace: issues and challenges in researching indigenous compensation claims. *Anthropological Forum, 28,* 255–274.

Partridge, J. C., Freeman, H., Weiss, E., & Martinez A. M. (2001). Delivery room resuscitation decisions for extremely low birthweight infants in California. *Journal of Perinatology, 21,* 27–33.

Paulhus, D. L. (1998). Interpersonal and intrapsychic adaptiveness of trait self-enhancement: A mixed blessing?. *Journal of Personality and Social Psychology, 74,* 1197–1208.

Payot, A., Gendron, S., Lefebvre, F., & Doucet, H. (2007). Deciding to resuscitate extremely premature babies: How do parents and neonatologists engage in the decision?. *Social Science and Medicine, 64,* 1487–1500.

Peat, D. (1921). *Synchronicity. The Bridge between Matter and Mind.* New York: Bantam Dell Group.

Phillips, M., & Frederick, C. (1992). The use of hypnotic age progressions as prognostic, ego-strengthening, and integrating technique. *American Journal of Clinical Hypnosis, 35,* 90–108.

Pile, S. (2009). Emotion and Affect in Recent Human Geography. *Transactions of the Institute of British Geographers, 35*(1), 5–20.

Pincus A. L., & Lukowitsky M. R. (2010). Pathological narcissism and narcissistic personality disorder. *Annual Review of Clinical Psychology, 2010*(6), 421–446.

Pincus A. L., Cain N. M., & Wright A. G. (2014). Narcissistic grandiosity and narcissistic vulnerability in psychotherapy. *Personality Disorders: Theory, Research, and Treatment, 5,* 439–443.

Porphyry. (1965). The life of Pythagoras. In Moses Hadas & Morton Smith (Eds.), *Heroes and Gods.* New York: Harper and Row, 105–128.

Post, J. M. (1984). Dreams of glory and the life cycle: Reflections on the life course of narcissistic leaders. *Journal of Political and Military Sociology, 12,* 49–60.

Post, J. M. (1986). Narcissism and the charismatic leader-follower relationship. *Political Psychology, 7,* 675–688.

Post, J. M. (1991). Saddam Hussein of Iraq: a political psychology profile. *Political Psychology, 12,* 279–289.

Post, J. M. (1993a). Current concepts of the narcissistic personality: Implications for political psychology. *Political Psychology, 14,* 99–121.

Post, J. M. (1993b). The defining moment of Saddam's life: A political psychology perspective on the leadership and decision making of Saddam Hussein during the Gulf crisis. In S. A. Renshon (Ed.), *The Political Psychology of The Gulf War: Leaders, Publics, and the Process of Conflict* (pp. 49–66). Pittsburgh: University of Pittsburgh Press.

Post, J. M., & Baram, A. (2003). "Saddam is Iraq: Iraq is Saddam" (until operation Iraqi freedom). In B. R. Schneider & J. M. Post (Eds.), *Know Thy Enemy: Profiles of Adversary Leaders and Their Strategic Cultures* (pp. 163–220). Maxwell Air Force Base, AL: USAF Counterproliferation Center.

Purdon, C., Antony, M. M., & Swinson, R. P. (1999). Psychometric properties of the Frost Multidimensional Perfectionism Scale in a clinical anxiety disorders sample. *Journal of Clinical Psychology, 55*(10), 1271–1286.

Raskin, R., & Novacek, J. (1991). Narcissism and the use of fantasy. *Journal of Clinical Psychology, 47*(4), 490–499.

Read, J., Cartwright, C., & Gibson, K. (2014). Adverse emotional and interpersonal effects reported by 1829 New Zealanders while taking antidepressants. *Psychiatry Research, 216*, 67–73.

Richards, D., & Richardson, T. (2012). Computer-based psychological treatments for depression: a systematic review and meta-analysis. *Clinical Psychology Review, 32*(4), 329–342.

Robins, R. W., & Beer, J. S. (2001). Positive illusions about the self: Short-term benefits and long-term costs. *Journal of Personality and Social Psychology, 80*, 340–352.

Roche M. J., Pincus A. L., Lukowitsky M. R., Ménard K. S., & Conroy D. E. (2013). An integrative approach to the assessment of narcissism. *Journal of Personality Assessment, 95*, 237–248.

Rockström, J., Steffen, W., Noone, K., Persson, Å., Chapin, F. S., III, Lambin, E. F., Lenton, T. M., Scheffer, M., Folke, C., Schellnhuber, H. J., Nykvist, B., de Wit, C. A., Hughes, T., van der Leeuw, S., Rodhe, H., Sörlin, S., Snyder, P. K., Costanza, R., Svedin, U., Falkenmark, M., Karlberg, L., Corell, R. W., Fabry, V. J., Hansen, J., Walker, B., Liverman, D., Richardson, K., Crutzen, P., & Foley, J. A. (2009). A safe operating space for humanity. *Nature, 461*, 472–475,

Roemer, L., & Borkovec, T. D. (1994). Effects of suppressing thoughts about emotional material. *Journal of Abnormal Psychology, 103*(3), 467–474.

Roemer, L., & Orsillo, S. M. (2005). An acceptance based behavior therapy for generalized anxiety disorder. In S. M. Orsillo & L. Roemer (Eds.), *Acceptance and mindfulness-based approaches to anxiety: Conceptualization and treatment* (pp. 213–240), New York: Springer.

Roemer, L., Orsillo, S., & Salters-Pedneault, K. (2009). Efficacy of an acceptance-based behavior therapy for generalized anxiety disorder: evaluation in a randomized controlled trial. *Journal of Consulting and Clinical Psychology, 76*, 1083–1089.

Roemer, L., Lee, J. K., Salters-Pedneault, K., Erisman, S. M., Orsillo, S. M., & Mennin, D. S. (2009). Mindfulness and emotion regulation difficulties in generalized anxiety disorder: Preliminary evidence for independent and overlapping contributions. *Behavior Therapy, 40*, 142–154.

Roscoe, L., & Schenck, D. (2017). *Communication and Bioethics at the End of Life: Real Cases, Real Dilemmas*. Holland: Springer.

Rosenthal S. A., & Pittinsky T. L. (2006). Narcissistic leadership. *The Leadership Quarterly, 17*, 617–633.

Rumbaut, R. G. (1997). Assimilation and its discontents: between rhetoric and reality. *The International Migration Review, 31*(4), 923–960.

Salice, A., & Miyazono K. (2020). Being one of us. *Philosophical Psychology, 33*, 42–63.

Sandell, K., & Bornäs, H. (2015). Functioning numbness instead of feelings as a direction: Young adults' experiences of antidepressant use. *Sociology, 3*, 130–147.

Sartre J.-P. (1996/1939). *A Sketch for a Theory of the Emotions*. London: Routledge.

Sartre J.-P. (1983/1940). *The Psychology of Imagination*. London: Methuen & Co.

Sartre J.-P. (1993/1943). *Being and Nothingness: An Essay on Phenomenological Ontology*. London: Routledge.

Sartre, J. P. (1957). *The Transcendence of the Ego* (Forrest Williams & George Kirkpatrick (Trans.). New York: Noonday Press.

Sartre, J-P. (1996/1939). *A sketch for a theory of the emotions*. London: Routledge.

Sartre, J. P. (2010). *Being and Nothingness*. Paris: Gallimard.

Scheler, (2008[1954]). *The Nature of Sympathy* (P. Heath. Trans.). New Brunswick, London: Transaction Publishers.

Schenk, D. P., & Roscoe, L. A. (2017). *Communication and bioethics at the end of life, real Cases. Real Dilemmas*. Holland: Springer.

Schmid, H. B. (2009). *Plural action. Essays in philosophy and social science*. Dordrecht: Springer.

Schmid, H. B. (2014a). Plural self-awareness. *Phenomenology and the Cognitive Sciences, 13*, 7–24.

Schmid, H. B. (2014b). The feeling of being a group. Corporate emotions and collective consciousness. In C. von Scheve & M. Salmela (Eds.), *Collective emotions* (pp. 3–16). Oxford: Oxford University Press.

Schneider, H. (2016). From community health workers to community health systems: Time to widen the horizon?. *Health Systems & Reform, 2*, 112–118.

Schutz, A. (1945). The homecomer. American Journal of Sociology, *50*(5) (Mar., 1945), 369–376.

Seamon, D., & Sowers, J. (2009). Existentialism/existential geography. In R. Kitchen & N. Thrift (Eds.), *The International Encyclopedia of Human Geography*, (Vol. 3, 666–671). Oxford: Elsevier.

Searle, J. (1990). Collective intentions and actions. In P. Cohen, J. Morgan, & M. E. Pollack (Eds.), *Intentions in Communication*. Cambridge, MA: Bradford Books, MIT Press.

Searle, J. (1995). *The Construction of Social Reality*. New York, N.Y.: Free Press.

Sedeño, L., Couto, B., Melloni, M., Canales-Johnson, A., Yoris, A., Baez, S., & Ibanez, A. (2014). How do you feel when you can't feel your body? Interoception, functional connectivity and emotional processing in depersonalization-derealization disorder. *PLoS One, 9*(6), e98769.

Sedikides, C., Rudich, E. A., Gregg, A. P., Kumashiro, M., & Rusbult, C. (2004). Are normal narcissists psychologically healthy?: self-esteem matters. *Journal of Personality and Social Psychology, 87*, 400–416.

Segal, Z. V., Williams, J. M. G., & Teasdale, J. D. (2002). *Mindfulness-based Cognitive Therapy for Depression: A New Approach to Preventing Relapse*. New York: Guilford Press.

Shaw, L. K., & Warf, B. (2009). Worlds of affect. *Environment and Planning*, A, *41*, 1332–1343.

Sibley, D. (1995) *Geographies of Exclusion*. London: Routledge.

Silverman, William A. (1993). Is neonatal medicine in the United States out of step?. *Pediatrics, 92*, 612–661.

Simeonov, P. L. (2015). Yet another time about time. Part I: An essay on the phenomenology of physical time, *PubMed, 119*(3), 271–287.

Simon, G., Ormel, J., VonKorff, M., & Barlow, W. (1995). Health care costs associated with depressive and anxiety disorders in primary care. *The American Journal of Psychiatry, 152*(3), 352–357.

Simpson, J. (1999). "Response to 'Neonatal viability in the 1990s: Held hostage by technology' by Jonathan Muraskas et al. and 'Giving moral distress a voice: Ethical concerns among neonatal intensive care unit personnel" (P. Heffernan, S. Heilig, Eds.) *Cambridge Quarterly Healthcare Ethics, 8*, 524–526.

Smith, S. J. (2000). Performing the (sound)world. *Society and Space, 18*, 615–637.

Smith, A., Anderson, M. (2018). "Social Media Use in 2018," Pew Research Center, published online first.

Smith, M., Davidson, J., & Henderson, V. L. (2012). Spiders, Sartre and 'magical geographies': the emotional transformation of space. *Transactions of the Institute of British Geographers*, *37*(1), 60–74.

Sorabji, R. (1993). Animal minds. *The Southern Journal of Philosophy*, *31*, 1–18.

Sousa, C. A., Kemp, S., & El-Zuhairi, M. (2014). Dwelling within political violence: palestinian women's narratives of home, mental health, and resilience. *Health Place*, *30*, 205–214.

Spiegel, D., Lulu, J., & Willson, S. (2017). *Dissociative amnesia. Merck Manual, Professional Version*. Kenilworth, NJ: Merck, Sharp & Dohme Corp.

Steffen, W., Broadgate, W., Deutsch, L., Gaffney, O., & Ludwig, C. (2015). The trajectory of the anthropocene: the great acceleration. *The Anthropocene Review*, *2*(1), 81–98.

Stein, E. (1922). Beiträge zur Philosophischen Begründung der Psychologie und der Geisteswissenschaften. Zweite Abhandlung: Individuum und Gemeinschaft. In E. Husserl (Ed.), Jahrbuch für Philosophie und Phänomenologische Forschung (Vol. 5, pp. 116–284). Halle: Max Niemeyer.

Strozier, C. B. (1983). Fantasy, self psychology and the inner logic of cults. In Goldberg, A. (Ed.), *The future of psychoanalysis*. New York: International Universities Press.

Sygminton, N. (1993). *Narcissism a New Theory*. London, Karmac.

Szanto, T. (2015). Collective emotions, normativity and empathy: a steinen account. *Journal of Human Studies*, *38*, 503–527.

Tarrier, N., Pilgrim, H., Sommerfield, C., Faragher, B., Reynolds, M., Graham, E., & Barrowclough, C. (1999). A randomized trial of cognitive therapy and imaginal exposure in the treatment of chronic posttraumatic stress disorder. *Journal of Consulting and Clinical Psychology*, *67*(1), 13–18.

Tartakoff, H. (1966). The normal personality in our culture and the Nobel Prize complex. In En Lowenstein, R. (Ed.), *Psychoanalysis: A General Psychology. Essays in Honor of Heinz Hartmann* (pp. 222–252). New York: International Universities Press.

Thompson, R. (1990). Emotion and self-regulation. *Nebraska Symposium on Motivation. Nebraska Symposium on Motivation, 36*, 367–467.

Thrift, N. (2004). Intensities of feeling: towards a spatial politics of affect *Geografiska Annaler, 86B*, 57–78.

Tillich, P. (1952a). *The Courage To Be*. New Haven: Yale University Press.

Tillich, P. (1952b). *Anxiety, Religion, and Medicine. Pastoral Psychology*. Holland: Springer.

Trujillo, Laura (2009). Ecología política del desarrollo sostenible. Unpublished document. Universidad Andina Simón Bolívar, document submitted in the doctoral course on Collective Health, Environment and Society.

Tschakert, Petra, & Tutu, Raymond (2010). *Environment, Forced Migration and Social Vulnerability* (pp. 57–69). Berlin, Heidelberg: Springer.

Tschakert, P., Tutu, R., & Alcaro, A. (2013). Embodied experiences of environmental and climatic changes in landscapes of everyday life in Ghana. *Emotion, Space and Society*, *7*, 13–25.

Twenge, J. M., & Campbell, W. K. (2010). *The Narcissism Epidemic: Living in the Age of Entitlement*. NY: First Free Press.

Twenge, J. M., Catanese, K. R., & Baumeister, R. F. (2003). Social exclusion and the deconstructed state: Time perception, meaninglessness, lethargy, lack of emotion, and self-awareness. *Journal of Personality and Social Psychology*, *85*, 409–423.

Twenge, J. M., Baumeister, R. F., Tice, D. M., & Stucke, T. S. (2001). If you can't join them, beat them: Effects of social exclusion on aggressive behavior. *Journal of Personality and Social Psychology*, *81*(6), 1058–1069.

Twenge, J. M., Konrath, S., Foster, J. D., Campbell, W. K., & Bushman, B. J. (2008). Egos inflating over time: A cross-temporal meta-analysis of the Narcissistic Personality Inventory. *Journal of Personality, 76,* 875–901.

Twenge, J., Zhang, L., Catanese, K., Dolan-Pascoe, B., Lyche, L., & Baumeister, R. (2007). Replenishing connectedness: reminders of social activity reduce aggression after social exclusion. *The British Journal of Social Psychology, 46,* 205–224.

Uchino, B. N., Cacioppo, J. T., & Kiecolt-Glaser, J. K. (1996). The relationship between social support and physiological processes: a review with emphasis on underlying mechanisms and implications for health. *Psychological Bulletin, 119*(3), 488–531.

Van Boven, L., & Loewenstein, G. (2003). Social projection of transient drive states. *Personality and Social Psychology Bulletin, 29*(9), 1159–1168.

Van Lange, O., DeBruin, J. (1997). Development of prosocial, individualistic, and competitive orientations: theory and preliminary evidence. *Journal of Personality and Social Psychology, 73*(4), 733–746.

Volkan, V. (1980). Narcissistic personality organization and reparative leadership. *International Journal of Group Psychotherapy, 30,* 131–152.

Volkan, V. (1982). Narcissistic personality disorder. In Cavenor, J. O. Brodie, H. K. (Eds.), *Critical Problems Psychiatry* (pp. 332–350). Philadelphia: J. B. Lippincott Co.

Volkan, V. (1988). *The need to have enemies and allies.* New York: Aronson.

Volkan, V., & Itzkowitz, N. (1984). *The immortal Atatürk.* Chicago: University of Chicago Press.

Wallace, H. M., & Baumeister, R. F. (2002). The performance of narcissists rises and falls with perceived opportunity for glory. *Journal of Personality and Social Psychology, 82*(5), 819–834.

Wandersman, A. H., & Hallman, W. K. (1993). Are people acting irrationally? Understanding public concerns about environmental threats. *American Psychologist, 48,* 681–686.

Warsini, S., Mills, J., & Usher, K. Solastalgia: living with the environmental damage caused by natural disasters. *Prehospital and Disaster Medicine, 29,* 87–90.

Watkins, J. G. (1971). The affect bridge: a hypnoanalytic technique. *The International Journal of Clinical and Experimental Hypnosis, XIX,* 21–27.

Watkins, J. G., & Watkins, H. H. (1987). *Ego States: Theory and Therapy.* New York: W. W. Norton.

Watson, D., Clark, L. A., & Tellegen, A. (1988). Development and validation of brief measures of positive and negative affect: The PANAS scales. *Journal of Personality and Social Psychology, 54*(6), 1063–1070.

Weber, A. *Matter and Desire.* White River Junction, Vermont: Chelsea Green Publishing.

Weems, Carl, Costa, Natalie, Dehon, Christopher, & Berman, Steven (2004). Paul Tillich's theory of existential anxiety: A preliminary conceptual and empirical examination. *Anxiety, Stress and Coping, 17,* 383–399.

Wegner, D. M. (1994). Ironic processes of mental control. *Psychological Review, 101*(1), 34–52.

Williams, K. D., Cheung, C. K. T., & Choi, W. (2000). Cyberostracism: Effects of being ignored over the Internet. *Journal of Personality and Social Psychology, 79*(5), 748–762.

Williams, K. D., Forgas, J. P., van Hippel, W. (2005). *The Social Outcast: Ostracism, Social Exclusion, Rejection, and Bullying.* New York: Psychology Press.

Wilson, M. S., & Sibley. C. G. (2011). 'Narcissism Creep?': Evidence for Age-Related Differences in Narcissism in the New Zealand General Population. *New Zealand Journal of Psychology, 40*(3), 89–95.

Wilson, T. D., Wheatley, T. P., Kurtz, J. L., Dunn, E. W., & Gilbert, D. T. (2004). When to Fire: Anticipatory Versus Postevent Reconstrual of Uncontrollable Events. *Personality and Social Psychology Bulletin, 30*(3), 340–351.

Wolpe, J. (1958). *Psychotherapy by Reciprocal Inhibition.* Palo Alto: Stanford Univer. Press.

Woodruff H. B. (2014). Selman A. Waksman, winner of the 1952 Nobel Prize for physiology or medicine. *Applied and environmental microbiology, 80*(1), 2–8. https://doi.org/10.1128/AEM.01143-13.

Wu, T. (2006). The World Trade Law of Censorship and Internet Filtering. *Chicago Journal of International Law,* 7(1), Article 1.

Wu, T. (2016). *The Attention Merchants.* New York: Knopf.

Yalom, I. D. (1980). *Existential psychotherapy.* Basic Books.

Young, D. J. (1992). Language anxiety from the foreign language specialist's perspective: Interviews with Krashen, Omaggio Hadley, Terrell, and Rardin. *Foreign Language Annals, 25,* 157–172.

Zadro, L., Williams, K. D., & Richardson, R. (2004). How low can you go? Ostracism by a computer is sufficient to lower self-reported levels of belonging, control, self-esteem, and meaningful existence. *Journal of Experimental Social Psychology, 40*(4), 560–567.

Zahavi, D. (2015). You, me, and we: the sharing of emotional experience. *Journal of Consciousness Studies, 22,* 84–101.

Zahavi, D. (2018) Collective intentionality and plural pre-reflective self-awareness. *Journal of Social Philosophy, 49,* 61–65.

Ziervogel, G. (2019). *Unpacking the Cape Town drought: Lessons learned,* available online.

Zinbarg, R. E., Barlow, D. H. (1996). Structure of anxiety and the anxiety disorders: A hierarchical model. *Journal of Abnormal Psychology, 105*(2), 181–193.

# APPENDIX

## Questionnaire

Name
Age
Profession
Nationality
Place where you grew up

- When did the phobia start?
- When was it at its peak?
- When was quite manageable?
- Can you recognize the feelings and sensations that prepare the raise of your fear and anxiety?
- How disruptive is your phobia at the moment?
- How would you describe that disruption?
- How often in a day/month/year do you avoid the possibility of being in contact with the object of your phobia?
- How often in a day/month/year do you avoid the possibility of thinking about the object of your phobia?
- How often in a day/month/year do you consciously choose to challenge your phobia?
- How often in a day/month/year do you feel ashamed of your phobia?
- If there are, what are the feeling sensations that accompany that?
- If there are, what are the thoughts that accompany that?
- How often in a day/month/year do you assume a judgmental stance in relation to your phobia?

- What are the words you use?
- If there are, what are the images or random associations that are associated with those judgments?
- How often do you feel compassionate toward yourself when a phobic thought or experience arises?
- If you feel any, how would you describe the feeling evoked by that compassionate act
- If there is any compassion, how would you describe the thoughts emerging from that act of compassion?
- Which one of these reactions you think could increase the quality of your life: self-compassion, self-shaming, self-blaming?
- What's the emotion that you would mostly associate to a phobic episode?
- What's the emotion that you would associate the least to a phobic episode?
- What are the emotions that you think prepare a phobic episode?
- What are the emotions that you think follow a phobic episode?
- How do you feel about exposure to your phobia?
- How do you feel about accepting your phobia?

# INDEX

For Product Safety Concerns and Information please contact our EU
representative  GPSR@taylorandfrancis.com
Taylor & Francis Verlag GmbH, Kaufingerstraße 24, 80331 München, Germany

www.ingramcontent.com/pod-product-compliance
Lightning Source LLC
Chambersburg PA
CBHW072311290326
41932CB00069B/3053

9 780367 674618